Th€ Cur$€ Of $kinwa£k€r Ranch

Simon Charles Smith

DEDICATION

To those who value truth above all else.

CONTENTS

SEASON TWO

APPENDICES AND INDEX

ACKNOWLEDGMENTS

Many thanks to Royce L Robertson and the rest of his colleagues for providing important insights on the nature of the Skinwalker Ranch scam. This book in no way presupposes Royce and the others will agree with all of my analysis or is representative of their own views. Thanks also to Winnie, my friend and Microsoft Word consultant. And last but not least my sister Sarah whose encouragement is like the gentle rain to we solitudeness flowers who presume to call ourselves *writers*...

PREFACE

The Curse of Skinwalker Ranch has huge following in the conspira-circus world. I watch it primarily on the *Blaze TV* channel here in the UK. It is made by *Prometheus Entertainment* then premiered on the ~~Hitler~~ *History Channel* before being syndicated elsewhere.

I'm currently writing a book on political economy. As a relaxation however, I watch a mix of programming on the channel, ranging from the excellent *The Curse of Oak Island* to accidental comedy such as *Ancient Aliens*.

Only later in series two of *The Curse Of Skinwalker Ranch* did the penny drop that my fascination with UFO and paranormal had a distinct economics angle above and beyond just being a merely another TV viewing *grift*. Although it must be said that most TV programming while nominally made for entertainment has a brainwashing function when applied to the public's psyche.

I must say, I like to detect deception as much as I like to be informed. This instinct has grown more, the older I get. Now, any thinking people will know *The Curse of Skinwalker Ranch* is nonsense, but what kind of nonsense is it, is the question.

The more I watched *The Curse of Skinwalker Ranch*, the more I was interested in solving the intellectual puzzle it was becoming for me. There are three type of people who will watch this show:

1/ Those wanting a new religion and salivate on their favourite characters.

2/ Those who will call rubbish very soon and give up watching fairly soon.

3/ And those like me who enjoy unravelling deception.

This book is not for groupies of older women who have ditched their boyband allegiance. They will scarcely be dissuaded from their soap opera lusting over Thomas Winterton or Travis Taylor. Nor will the *sub-basement* dwelling *half truthers* find comfort in these pages. Indeed, I'm reminded of the film *Inherit The Wind* based on the *Scopes Monkey Trial* where the defence attorney played by Spencer Tracey tells his client that his *real crime* was destroying the townsfolks' dreams.[1]

I suppose I am destroying the groupies and half-truthers' dreams. If I see a mob of middle women and geeks gathering outside my apartment with torches and pitchforks led by Travis Taylor then I guess I was wrong about who my readers might be.

I mean, who doesn't want to live in a world of real life heroes braving attacks from skinwalkers while investigating paranormal behaviour and UFOs?

Who wants to watch and fully acknowledge the pseudo non-fiction it really is? Good grief; how are normal hardworking stressed out people to find relief from their daily grind, financial hardships, and family arguments etc.?

By the same token those changing channels fairly soon after watching the show will regard my attempt at deconstruction as a sledgehammer to crack a nut. They too will not read my book. After all why would the US government allow a private owner to allow filming and investigation of phenomena that would have defence implications?

I know, a ridiculous suspension of disbelief is necessary...

No, this book is written for people in the third category. This will be a minority for sure. And for this other category of sceptics, let me ~~plug~~ recommend my previous book of a similar genre: *Fake Aliens And The Phony Nuke World Order*.

Please see the referenced links for further information.[2, 3]

I HAVE POSTED LINKS ON MY WEBSITE: FAKEALIENSANDPHONYNUKES.COM TO FACILITATE EASIER ACCESS TO LINKS FOR THOSE PEOPLE WHO HAVE BOUGHT THE PAPERBACK VERSION OF THIS BOOK.

***

This book is not intended to derail Brandon Fugal and the others' real estate ~~seam~~ appreciation schemes. I doubt it will make much difference. People with their head screwed on — *a minority* — will already have comprehended the nature of the business. In a strange way I wish them well. They just want to create an Area 51-Roswell hybrid. At least they aren't engaged in a worldwide deception about a non-existent virus.

I considered calling this book *The Curse of Skingrifter Ranch*, but I maintain, unlike other fayre put out by the *History Channel* this has another dimension to it. It is not just a grift for the film producers. If I am correct, its remit is to increase tourism and hence elevate land prices in the Uintah Basin next to Skinwalker Ranch. It represents an unholy alliance between the quasi documentary makers and real estate interests. So, yes, it is a conspiracy against the public, but the last couple of years have seen far worse.

I believe we can apply statement analysis — see Appendix C — to discern the intentions of Brandon Fugal. This exchange is also included in Appendix B and in my opinion is a major smoking gun. Fugal responds to the interviewers question:

People have speculated that you are trying to develop a 'paranormal retreat' or a tourist destination.

Really? That isn't going to happen. The ranch isn't some place for ghost hunters to get their jollies. It's a serious scientific endeavor that requires patience and humility, and I have committed significant resources dedicated to discovering the truth of what is really happening. <u>What a silly idea.</u>

There is <u>zero intention to monetize it in any way</u>, although we do have traditional ranching activities such as raising cattle.

This book will attempt other statement analysis; suffice to say it seems a case of, *the lady doth protest too much, methinks...* or what a statement analyst might call *demonstrating a certain sensitivity* to the question being asked.

***

The road to deciphering *The Curse of Skinwalker Ranch* saw me changing back and forth on my opinion of who was in on the deception. For most of my viewing time I believed it was just a more sanitised version of *Ancient Aliens*; a deception yes, but a one dimensional deception.

I also wondered whether Erik Bard might have been point operative for outside *men in black* with microwave and gamma technology that were targeting the team. I supposed that information about where everybody was and when rocket where going to be launched would be a prerequisite for phenomena to be activated.

I entertained the idea that as such, the show may have been used as advertising for international arms dealers. A crazy idea or a *crazeee* idea as Travis Taylor would say. Gradually I came round to the realisation that they were all telling lies.

I do not bear any malice towards any of the Skinwalker team, and I hope they bear me none. This book is a companion for like-minded people such as myself.

1/ Inherit The Wind
https://www.imdb.com/title/tt0053946/

2/ My website
http://fakealiensandphonynukes.com/

3/ Links to this book
http://fakealiensandphonynukes.com/skinwalker.html

INTRODUCTION

The television series, *The Curse of Skinwalker Ranch* is a hotchpotch of narrative about skinwalkers, UFOs, portals, and other *strange phenomena*. It builds upon a canon that includes, but is not limited to, the pseudo non-fiction books of Ryan Skinner and *Hunt For The Skinwalker: Science Confronts The Unexplained At A Remote Ranch In Utah*, written by George Knapp and Colm Kelleher.

Attendant grifters on Facebook have also provided Skinwalker motifed teeshirts for those wishing to worship at the altar of the Skinwalker without enduring the onerous task of reading a book.

So, from the point of view of its overall money making appeal, Skinwalker Ranch material has become a cottage industry. Skinwalker Ranch is a non-urban myth, built on echo chambers, hearsay, and pure fabrication. It is more of a study of mass psychosis formation than of aliens and skinwalkers.

The show is put out by *Prometheus Entertainment*. Here is what their *about us* message says:[1]

Established in 1999, Prometheus Entertainment has been a leader in supplying critically acclaimed, highly-rated programming to the cable marketplace. The company has produced over 900 hours of dynamic and diverse television for clients such as History, A&E, E!, WEtv, Travel Channel, Bravo, Animal Planet, Lucasfilm Ltd., National Geographic Channel, AMC, Warner Bros -- and more.

From top-rated docudramas such as "THE CURSE OF OAK ISLAND", "THE GIRLS NEXT DOOR", and "KENDRA," and to imaginative and informative non-fiction series and specials such as "ANCIENT ALIENS," "AMERICA'S BOOK OF SECRETS," "FOOD PARADISE" and "STAR WARS: THE LEGACY REVEALED," Prometheus Entertainment consistently provides programs that inform, provoke and always entertain.

And for what it's worth, assuming it is genuine I hope — I will forgive a little scripting — *The Curse of Oak Island* is one of my all-time favourite documentaries. It seems that while *Prometheus Entertainment* is separate from the *History Channel*, it is closely associated. The *History Channel* is part of *A & E Networks*. Wikipedia informs us:[2]

A&E was formed from the merger of the Alpha Repertory Television Service and the Entertainment Channel, a premium cable channel, in 1984 with their respective owners keeping stakes in the new company. Thus A&E's shareholders were Hearst and ABC (from ARTS) and Radio City Music Hall (Rockefeller Group) and RCA, then the parent of NBC (from Entertainment Channel). The company launched Arts & Entertainment Network, a cultural cable channel, on February 1, 1984.

From the perspective of *Prometheus Entertainment* and the *History Channel, The Curse Of Skinwalker Ranch* is a pure money making from entertainment exercise. In some ways this makes it quite innocent. As Samuel Johnson once said:

There are few ways in which a man can be more innocently employed than in getting money.

But are viewers being deceived beyond that suspension of belief that the programme makers have a moral right to intrude beyond?

I maintain there is an extra agenda in play above and beyond successful television programming. This is the rollout of a tourist initiative with *Skinwalker Ranch* being an *Area 51-Roswell* style development that seeks to develop the area's economy beyond that of its traditional farming and partially realised mineral resources. In so far as this initiative is followed, the confidence trick played on the rest of the world may benefit the Utah economy and especially the landholding classes.

***

I want to start off by recommending, or even not recommending, a way to read this book. First of all, I hope it is a given the reader has watched some if not most of the shows?

After this introduction and a lengthy but interesting prologue, the book is divided into three main sections: *Series One Episodes, Series Two Episodes*, and the *Appendices*. Living in the UK, I have not yet had the opportunity to watch season three. I expect when I do, it will be more of the same.

The reader might like to match his or her

own viewing notes while watching a particular episode of *The Curse Of Skinwalker Ranch* with my own. All chess players will understand that when a chess position is given as puzzle to be solved, the analysis can be found on another page. By analogy the reader might like to attempt this on occasion to see if they agree with my analysis.

Notwithstanding, I'm up front with my beliefs about the show right from the start. Conclusions that were firmed up as episode nine series two came to an end. As such, my approach isn't the unfolding week by week soap opera narrative that keeps people spellbound, but I drench the reader in a bucket of cold water right from the start. The unfolding promise of revelation that is promised from week to week but never realised is part of the drug dealer's allure; it is part immature humanity's ever expectancy of deliverance in the future, but actually, *the kingdom of God is at hand...*

The appendices complement the episodes. Please take time to over a general overview, and by all means leave the episode in question to view information about *statement analysis, the players, and maps etc*. Not for the first time I mention that the problem with a book as opposed to a painting is its linearity. There are many facets to this interesting puzzle that deserved to be viewed overall.

Understanding is more important than just reading from page one to the end. It goes without saying that a critical reading of my book will have the reader saying, *I don't agree with that*; great, take a pencil and scribble over the page where you disagree; I do it all the time with many authors I otherwise really appreciate and consequently recommend.

Introduction

The division of the first two seasons is further delineated by the observation that the first series gave dates, but the second series didn't. From the point of view of the student of BS, the changing of format was something of a giveaway of untruthful intent. I daresay that *Prometheus Entertainment,* if they were to do it all again, would omit dates from their timestamping of the first season.

I have written several appendices: *Appendix A – Maps, Photos, And Shadows*; *Appendix B – The Cast Of Players; Appendix C – Statement Analysis; Appendix D – Facebook And Fandom; Appendix E – Skinwalker Ranch Is A Grift;* and *Appendix F – Discrepancies In Canon.* I suggest a certain skim reading of the appendices may help in the episode by episode chapter guides. This may not be a book to read through all at once, but it is absolutely necessary to watch the episodes to appreciate my commentary as I expect 99% of my readers to have done anyway.

The various players have interesting backgrounds and relationships. For example, who would have known that Bryant *Dragon* Arnold and Brandon Fugal were Mormon missionaries together; that Travis Taylor has in common with Robert Bigelow an association with the University of Alabama while Brandon Fugal and Robert Bigelow are both real estate guys.

Statement analysis is a discipline brought to my attention by Peter Hyatt who has written about how it is possible to detect deceit by the way people speak or write. In many ways this is the most interesting part of the Skinwalker production for those of us who delight in taking apart deception.

Since *The Curse of Skinwalker Ranch* is akin to a soap opera, certain themes do crop up time and time again. The *dig no-dig debate*, once again involving a triangle of interactions between Brandon Fugal, Bryant Arnold, and Travis Taylor, is a recurrent theme.

***

I need to now say how I have documented the episodes. *The Curse of Skinwalker Ranch's* producers are able to avail themselves of copious amount of editing and splicing together non-sequential film to finish up with non-contiguous elements in order to develop a coherent consistent narrative. In my episode deconstruction, I needed to show how a player may be speaking in the present moment of action filming then have his subsequent after the fact reflections incorporated with the presented existential flow.

When a player is reflecting upon events, I have decided to indicate this explicitly by describing the person as making an *aside*. My aesthetic preference is for recording direct dialogue as italics rather than enclosing it within quotation marks. I do, however, use quotation marks when a someone writes or speaks about what someone else says to provide a further layer of nesting...

1 Prometheus Entertainment
http://www.Prometheus
Entertainmententertainment.com/

2 A & E Networks
https://en.wikipedia.org/wiki/A%26E_Networks#Chan
nels

PROLOGUE

It is the book written by George Knapp and Colm Kelleher, *Hunt For The Skinwalker: Science Confronts The Unexplained At A Remote Ranch In Utah* that has been responsible to a large degree in catapulting Skinwalker Ranch to national and international fame.

I must say that I read this book with low expectations. The truth is, it is very well written, engaging, but mostly fabricated lies. In this it matches the TV series that has sought to further amplify the BS. In many ways the Bigelow era of ownership is much more interesting than the Fugal era of ownership. Since the Fugal ownership is the mainstay of the *Th€ Cur$€ of $kinwa£k€r Ranch,* the reader might think *darn, I should have looked at the Bigelow era.*

Nevertheless, deconstruction of the Fugal era is still interesting for those of us of a particular mindset, and like it or not, what happened — or didn't happen — on Bigelow's watch, provides background for trying to understand the current TV show.

I've come to regard Knapp and Kelleher's book and the TV series as the as the *Old* and *New Testaments* of the Skinwalker cult. One interesting aspect of apprehending religious text study is how to explain — indeed if it can be done at all — discrepancies in canon. I have included these in *Appendix F – Discrepancies In Canon*. Now, if there are huge discrepancies this means:

The Knapp-Kelleher book is fabricated, or the TV series is bogus, or both. That the TV series is factual but the book is fabricated is impossible since the show attempts to use *Hunt For The Skinwalker* as canon. In other words, the *Old* and *New Skinwalker* may be false or the *Old* is true and the *New* false, but it is impossible for the TV show to be factual and the book to be a fabrication. As it happens, I believe both to be works of fiction.

***

I expect most of my readers have seen some or all of the TV episodes. As such they will be familiar with how the ranch was owned for many years by the Myers who then sold it to the Shermans. The Shermans previous to their admitted ownership were given the nom de plume of the *Gormans*. I will preserve this designation when quoting from the Knapp-Kelleher book. The book was published in 2006, long before Brandon Fugal purchased the ranch.

As an overall impression of the book compared to the TV series, there is a great deal of asymmetry with regard to strange phenomena. Either this is because the skinwalker-paranormal entities-ET aliens etc react differently over time to different people, or the means by which to fabricate narrative depends on whether one is using the printed word or a camera.

The books' authors provide what even they call a laundry list of strange phenomena including the likes of: Big Foot, *bullet proof wolves*, yellow orbs, orange orbs, red orbs, blue orbs, Schwarzenegger *Predator* like creatures, poltergeists, portals, and cattle mutilations. And it is these cattle mutilations I want to examine a little, as I believe they may be the key to understanding what happened on Bigelow's watch. But first I want to provide an account of the Myers' ownership of the ranch which contradicts both the TV series and the Knapp-Kelleher book. John and Edith Myers bought the ranch in 1933 and occupied it for sixty years.

These are a few abstracts from a link I provide here that in turn quotes Frank B Salisbury's, *The Utah UFO Display*, where the author interviews John Myer's brother, Garth: [1]

FBS: What about the important statement that the "greatest concentration of high strangeness has always taken place at what became the [Skinwalker] 480 - acre ranch?" Garth Myers vigorously denies it! Here are the important parts of the interview that I recorded:

Garth: I can tell you right off that my brother died in April of 1987. My sister-in-law lived alone there until about 1992. She died in March 1994. And I can tell you unequivocally that up to 1992 there had never been and there never were any signs of that UFO and similar activity.

Now, the ranch was vacant for about two years after she [entered a rest home]. I went to it occasionally just to check the house. Then we sold it to [the witness (Terry Sherman)] about six months after she died [actually, about three months]. I don't know what happened while it was vacant, but I don't think anything went on.

There was nothing, unequivocally, absolutely nothing that went on while she and my brother lived there. She lived there alone from 1987 to 1992, five years. And part of the time she had a dog. Before my former brother died; he had a dog that got caught in a trap and had one hind leg partially amputated. He lived for about three years, and then she was alone without a dog...."

FBS: I think that they make a statement in the book [Hunt for Skinwalker] that things had been going on since way back to the Indians, and so on. Garth: See, this is [the witness (Terry Sherman)]. That's the story he made. But it's not the right story!

Later, I called Garth Myers from the Uintah Basin to ask him a few more questions. First is the matter of locks inside and outside the house when the witness bought it. Garth has said that this simply was not true. When he visited the ranch, it took one key to enter the home, and if that key didn't work, a sharp kick on the door would let him in! There was no profusion of locks. (The witness, however, told me that there were small sliding locks on cupboards inside.)

Second is the matter of no digging being allowed on the ranch. That rumor might have been fortified by Charles Winn, who said he was digging something for Kenneth Myers with his backhoe when Kenneth told him for sure not to dig in a certain area. That doesn't sound very sinister. If I owned a ranch, I might not want someone with a backhoe to dig in certain places. So what? Garth said that the only stipulation in the real estate contract was that the previous owners retained the oil rights to the property! Since oil has become important in the Basin, such a stipulation is

*common when a ranch is sold. So the real-estate
contract stipulated that if the new owners dug for
oil, they must notify the previous owners. Does this
sound like "a meaningless clause crafted by elderly
eccentrics"?*

*...We had a long conversation with John
Garcia (called Mr. Gonzalez in Skinwalker), whose
ranch adjoined the Myers/(Skinwalker) ranch on
the cast, and with Charles Winn, whose ranch
adjoined it on the northwest. Each rancher had
some wonderful UFO stories to tell, as I'll relate at
the end of this chapter, but again and again we
asked if this activity occurred while the Myers were
living on the property. Time and again they would
search back in their memories and come up blank
as to activity on the ranch before the Myers left.
Garcia's account, the one related below, did go back
to the Myers' time, but he didn't think the Myers
were aware of his sighting.*

*Except for Garcia's account and various
cattle mutilations, most of the Garcia and Winn
stories were generated by experiences after Robert
Bigelow bought the ranch. The cattle mutilations
were confirmed by Pete Pickup, who had been a
deputy sheriff and a tribal policeman starting
during the Myers' occupancy. He had investigated
at least a dozen cattle mutilations at various
ranches, going back to the 1970s, and he was
employed by NIDS and Bob Bigelow, but he could
not confirm UFO activity prior to the witness's
purchase of the ranch.*

I refer the reader to Salisbury's book and the
linked website for more detail. Suffice to say we have
learnt from him that contrary to the science fiction
like accounts on the prohibition upon digging and
poltergeist behaviour, there were no extraordinary

events experienced in over sixty years. But the possibility that cattle mutilations are associated with the following Sherman-Bigelow era is in itself interesting.

***

I don't think anyone could disagree that George Knapp and Colm Kelleher have provided something of a public relations function for Robert Bigelow. I am not a fan of George Knapp. I believe he is a man who operates on the cusp of intelligence and big business, mediated by the mainstream media. That Wikipedia describes him as an investigative journalist suggests they like him.[2] Wikipedia also describes Linda Moulton Howe as an investigative journalist and only as an *advocate* of conspiracy theories.[3] Of course the title of *conspiracy theorist* at the start of someone's Wikipedia entry is the most damning from those guardians of establishment doctrine. Bill Cooper's entry on Wikipedia describes him as a *conspiracy theorist*; they don't like him.[4]

Why am I mentioning this?

Because George Knapp's comparison between Bob Lazar and Bill Cooper deserves some attention. According to Wikipedia:

Knapp reported on the story of Bob Lazar, who claimed to have worked on extraterrestrial UFOs at the secretive Area 51. According to Knapp, his discovery of evidence corroborating some of Lazar's claims made his stories on Lazar be taken more seriously than typical UFO fare. In 1990, Knapp's stories on Lazar earned an "Individual Achievement by a Journalist" award from the United Press International. However, to Knapp's "eternal shame," he also during this era publicized the claims of conspiracy theorist Bill Cooper, whom

Knapp came to regard as far less credible than Lazar.

We have no reason to doubt this estimation from the establishment propaganda machine. I am familiar with both Cooper and Lazar through my own UFO research. While Cooper was often wrong, and he himself would admit it, his heart was in the right place in my opinion. Lazar is a downright liar. I give reasons for this in *Fake Aliens And The Phony Nuke World Order*. For what's it's worth, the late ufologist Stanton Friedman thought him to be a fraud as well – although I'm no fan of Friedman.

I don't want to dwell on the Lazar case at any length, suffice to say Lazar's reference to *Zeta Reticula* ironically was based on the poor investigation of the Betty and Barney Hill case by Friedman where the *home of the grey aliens* was deduced from a suspect hypnotic remembering of a star chart. Friedman, like other investigators, has shown Lazar's educational claims are bogus. Lazar has been convicted of keeping a brothel. I'm even more convinced Lazar is a fraud than a few years back. Anyone who champions Lazar as genuine must surely be looked at quite closely themselves.

George Knapp was part of the corporate west's team when the Soviet Union was being dismantled. He was given an inside track to military figures in order to report on UFOs from beyond the former iron curtain. For those who don't know, the Soviet Union was carved up by a combination of Russian oligarchs and Wall Street while the ordinary people were disenfranchised from the means of production that the communist dream failed to deliver upon.

I refer the interested reader to the works of Antony Sutton on the East-West relationship.

Suffice to say, the Cold War was a complete theatrical production. But the whole world is a stage...

You do not get to grace our television screens as a journalist unless you are a whore of the corporations. This is very clear now in light of the covid scamdemic, but twenty years ago it was not so clear that mainstream journalists were hired guns. George Knapp does a very good impersonation as a *man of the people.* He oozes confidence in a bombastic well-groomed earnest overpowering way that takes many people in. Like all expert disinformationalists, he will be right on the things that can be verified and wrong on the things he is paid to mislead on. Let us examine the preface of *Hunt For The Skinwalker,* to see what Knapp says of himself:

<u>A scientist or mainstream journalist who decides to give serious consideration to unidentified flying objects or other so-called paranormal topics does so at considerable risk to his or her professional standing.</u> I learned this the hard way. In my twenty-five years as an investigative reporter, TV anchorman, and newspaper columnist in one of the world's most dynamic cities, I have been fortunate to cover stories large and small. I've tangled with Mafia figures, professional hitmen, casino moguls, crooked politicians, drug dealers, gunrunners, car bombers, arsonists for hire, porn kings, outlaw motorcycle gangs, dirty cops, illegal polluters, animal abusers, bagmen, con men, scam artists, pimps, perverts, and scumbags of every stripe. <u>In my own community, I'm generally regarded as a serious journalist.</u> I mention this not as a boast but as a reference point.

I have underlined the points of most interest. The rest is a series of boasts. I concede there was a time over forty years ago say that compromised a mainstream figure's reputation by association with UFOs. Not so much these days or even fifteen years ago when the book was written. In this Knapp is being disingenuous. But significantly for the truth-seeker, the fact that he regards himself as *mainstream* pretty much condemns him.

***

I want to turn now to Colm Kelleher. Amazon's biography section on Kelleher deserves repeating:

Since obtaining his PhD in biochemistry from the University of Dublin Trinity College, Colm Kelleher has spent 35 years of his working life in a wide variety of diverse careers. Between 1991-1996, he was an immunology research scientist at the National Jewish Center in Denver Colorado.

Between 1996-2004, Kelleher led the National Institute for Discovery Science (NIDS) team on Skinwalker Ranch as well as multiple other NIDS projects. From 2004-2008, Colm served as laboratory director at San Francisco biotechnology company Prosetta where he led teams of scientists in executing DoD contracts to discover drugs against Ebola virus, Rift Valley Fever Virus, Junin, Machupo, Marburg and other viruses of interest to DoD.

In 2008 Kelleher became deputy administrator of Bigelow Aerospace Advanced Space Studies (BAASS) where he led the day-to-day operations in executing the AAWSAP contract with Defense Intelligence Agency (DIA).

From 2012-2020, Kelleher led the Environmental Control and Life Support Systems

(ECLSS) Department at Bigelow Aerospace. where he managed eleven separate projects that cumulatively resulted in the building of life support systems for expandable spacecraft in Low Earth Orbit (LEO).

Kelleher is author of Brain Trust (Simon & Schuster) and he co-authored Hunt for the Skinwalker in 2005 with award winning journalist George Knapp.

The background to his 2004 book, *Brain Trust: The Hidden Connection Between Mad Cow and Misdiagnosed Alzheimer's Disease* is worth reproducing as well:

When the cattle-borne sickness known as Mad Cow Disease first appeared in America in 2003, authorities were quick to assure the nation that the outbreak was isolated, quarantined, and posed absolutely no danger to the general public. What we were not told was that the origins of the sickness may already have been here and suspected for a quarter of a century.

This illuminating exposé of the threat to our nation's health reveals for the first time how Mad Cow Disease (a.k.a. Bovine Spongiform Encephalopathy) has jumped species, infecting humans in the form of Creutzfeldt-Jakob Disease (CJD), and may be hidden in the enormous increase in the number of Alzheimer's cases since 1979.

Detailing the history and biology of Mad Cow Disease, Brain Trust discloses how an investigation into the mysterious deaths in a group of cannibals in a remote part of the world evolved into a research program in the United States that may have had unforeseen and frightening consequences.

Prologue

The shocking questions examined include:
• Have millions of Americans already been exposed
to the prions known to cause Mad Cow Disease
through   years   of   eating   tainted   beef?
• Does the epidemic of prion disease spreading like
wildfire through the nation's deer and elk pose a
threat   to   hunters   and   venison   eaters?
• Are the cattle mutilations discovered in the last 30
years part of a covert, illegal sampling program
designed to learn how far the deadly prions have
spread throughout the nation's livestock and beef
products?

Exposing the devastating truth about Mad
Cow Disease and a new theory of the possible
consequences of a little-known government
research program and the potential national health
catastrophe that may be the result, Brain Trust
inoculates Americans with an effective cure: the
truth.

I point the reader towards the speculation
about cattle mutilations and prions in this earlier
book of his. A search on the term *prions* in *Hunt For
The Skinwalker* however, reveals zero entries. When
we examine the Frank Salisbury interview with
respect to mutilations prior and after the Sherman-
Bigelow ownership might we not speculate that
Bigelow's NIDS team were actually involved with
cattle mutilations themselves, and that Kelleher was
their leader; that in fact Kelleher is involved in
monumental chutzpah?

All this is speculation on my part. I reiterate
that the deconstruction of Bigelow's ownership is
more interesting than the deconstruction of Fugal's
ownership. Knapp-Kelleher write in chapter ten:

Then in winter of 1994–95, some very weird
things began to happen to his cattle....

What could have lifted a thousand pound cow in full flight off the ground in the middle of a vicious snowstorm? Gorman knew that most helicopters couldn't do it...

Over the next few months, another four animals just disappeared. Tom's stress level had climbed dramatically as a result. By April 1995, the very long winter had ended and the heavy rains had begun...

So, the mutilations start after the Shermans — aka *Gormans* — buy the ranch. Once again, no reports from the Myers' ownership. *Gorman knew that most helicopters couldn't do it...*

So Sherman is an expert on what a helicopter can lift is he?

Later on there are reports of a cow with broken legs that seem more consistent with a helicopter than a flying saucer. I do not argue against the appearance of deep state antigravity craft as part of the overall psyop aspect of the operation, but I do believe helicopters were more often used. That the authors deemphasise helicopters suggest they wish to emphasise antigravity, and in the mainstream indoctrination process we are always meant to conflate antigravity propulsion with ETs.

The authors describe a classical cattle mutilation:

The heifer was lying motionless, and her entire rear end had been carved out with what looked like an extremely sharp instrument. Gorman came galloping up at the sound of his son's panicked yells. His face turned ashen when he jumped into the canal with his son. There was no blood in the stream. The cut was flawless. It looked as if a six-inch-diameter, perfectly circular saw with a sucking device had jammed into the heifer's rear end and effortlessly sucked out the entire insides of the animal without any loss of blood. And it had happened right in the middle of a heavy rainstorm...

Tom had heard the phrase "cattle mutilation" before but had dismissed it as the fanciful campfire stories of bored cowboys. He took it very seriously now. He searched the banks of the canal for footprints or tracks, but he knew the heavy rains would have obscured them in a matter of minutes...

This idea that Sherman regarded mutilations as *fanciful*, I find hard to believe. Indeed the book states:

But Tom's problems with cattle mutilations, although economically devastating, were not unique. They had been widespread throughout the western states, and many eastern states, since the early 1970s...

And in chapter ten:

In the 1970s, in addition to the scores of cases in northeastern Colorado, hundreds, perhaps thousands, of animal mutilation reports were investigated by local law enforcement with cases occurring in fifteen states, from Minnesota and South Dakota and Montana to New Mexico and Texas...

Not a single person has been caught or charged in the entire thirty-five year history of the phenomenon...

So one has to wonder whether this is because the mutilators have friends in high places who can cover for them and have the leisure time to write books on the subject.

In fact, the Uinta Basin became such a hotbed of cattle mutilation in the 1970s that well-

known mutilation investigator Carl Whiteside from the Colorado Bureau of Investigation even made it a practice to take the trip across the Utah-Colorado border in a helicopter to land near felled animals in farmers' fields. Local ranchers in the Uinta Basin still talk about the Colorado investigative team's unbelievable rudeness and obnoxious behavior. And what was their diagnosis after investigating multiple cases? Predators. But a small number of veterinarians who have had the courage to go to the scene of the mutilations and investigate the cause of death tend to rule out the predator-scavenger theory in favor of something much more sinister...

But by and large, the focused decimation of a single herd is unusual. Gorman may have been relatively atypical in having so many registered animals mutilated or missing over a fifteen-month period. But the consequences to the Gorman family were both economically and psychologically devastating. They were being harassed on their own property by a ruthless and unseen enemy...

So, it is not credible that Sherman believed mutilations were fanciful. This is narrative building. Just like later in the TV series when Travis Taylor said he didn't believe in UFOs until he saw them; this too is BS. The book is interesting because it gives an example of a mutilation attempt gone wrong that actually confounds the theme of the book. From chapter thirteen:

The old rancher described going out to his eight-year-old cow and finding that she had two broken legs. Alarmed, he ran back inside to get a blanket to cover the shivering animal. The cow was obviously suffering and in shock. He suspected he might have to put her down.

Prologue

Gonsalez was astonished when he returned with the blanket five minutes later to discover that the animal was gone. He looked everywhere but couldn't find her. The field was an open pasture with no rocks or trees behind which an animal could hide. Yet in the space of a few minutes, in daylight, a cow with two broken legs had vanished. An hour later he looked out his window. It was now afternoon.

He told me he nearly fainted when he saw the cow lying in the same field but about fifty yards from her original position. He ran out to the suffering animal and examined her closely. This time all four legs were broken. He ran inside to get his gun and quickly put the poor animal out of its misery. After thinking long and hard about this bizarre incident, <u>Gonsalez concluded that the animal must have twice been lifted into some aircraft and twice been dropped into the field. Each time two of her legs had been broken. This was the only explanation that seemed to fit the facts. We didn't argue with him.</u>

In Mark Pilkington's most excellent *The Mirage Men,* he informs us of Gabe Valdez, a law enforcement officer who took an interest in cattle mutilations:

Back in the 1970s, Valdez's investigations had focused on the ranch of Manual Gomez, whose cattle had suffered particularly badly; alongside dead and mutilated animals he'd found caterpillar tracks, bits of paper, measuring tools, syringes, needles and a gas mask. One site was covered with radar-reflecting chaff, some of it stuffed into the dead cow's mouth. Some of the animals had broken bones and what appeared to be rope marks on their limbs, suggesting that they had been hoisted up then dropped back on to the ground. Whoever was doing this to the cattle, they were organized, and human.

Returning again to Kelleher, who acquaints himself with Gabe Valdez, he writes in chapter twenty one of the Dulce area of New Mexico:

I first met Valdez in 1997 when he came to work for the National Institute for Discovery Science. As a parallel project with the Gorman ranch, he and I spent about one hundred days in Dulce. The object of the exercise was to investigate the alleged anomalies that had made Dulce legendary. Valdez had by then retired from law enforcement and was only too happy to continue the investigations with NIDS....

Over the span of two years, Valdez and I conducted more than seventy interviews with Dulce residents and cataloged a stunning variety of anomalies that had never before seen the light of day...

On the basis of Valdez being a genuine investigator, I can't help think Kelleher is keeping a potential enemy closer — *à la the Godfather* — to himself than his friends. I speculate that from his own perspective, Kelleher is running a counter intelligence operation. My intuition is aided by the fact that as a local organiser of a small political party, I discovered that my line manager was an MI5 employee. I wrote about this in *Covid 1984 Cornwall 2020*. Suffice to say that once you have been conned in this way, you become very sensitive to counter intelligence elsewhere.

Kelleher writes of the final account of cattle losses:

In the space of eighteen to twenty months, someone or something had killed or stolen fourteen registered cattle out of a herd of eighty animals, an attrition rate approaching 20 percent. Each of the animals was worth a couple of thousand dollars. Economically, the family was devastated.

***

I want to turn now to Bigelow. It would be possible to write a whole book on him. The legend is that his fascination with space exploration led him to making lots of money in real estate in order to realise to attempt realising ambitions in this area. Believe that if you will. This is one internet journalist's take on Robert Bigelow:[5]

This whole "Alien, Skinwalker, Phony Research" scam has been going on for years and years.
NOW, IT HAS PRETTY MUCH MORPHED INTO A RELIGION WHOSE ACCOLYTES ATTACK WHEN ASKED TO PROVIDE ACTUAL DOCUMENTED, PROVABLE EVIDENCE.
Anne Victoria Clark
Dec 18, 2017
This Aliens Thing is a Total Scam
Look, I hate to be this guy, but I was born this guy. On Saturday, the New York Times ran a feature on the Pentagon's UFO program, and everyone got excited. A completely normal reaction to the news that there might be alien alloys in a building in Las Vegas.
And sure, I do think there are probably aliens out there, somewhere. Though if an advanced race of technologically superior aliens do exist, I hope they're too busy enjoying their universal basic income and 5,000Gbps wifi speed to worry about flying around our cornfields at night. Unless we're like some kind of backwater rest stop for the universe and they're just passing through for

the McDonald's. I would understand that.

But guys, this program is not about aliens. It's not about aliens at all. This program is about this:

The shadowy program — parts of it remain classified — began in 2007, and initially it was largely funded at the request of Harry Reid, the Nevada Democrat who was the Senate majority leader at the time and who has long had an interest in space phenomena. Most of the money went to an aerospace research company run by a billionaire entrepreneur and long-time friend of Mr. Reid's, Robert Bigelow, who is currently working with NASA to produce expandable craft for humans to use in space.

So, for those of you not familiar with how defense spending works, basically congress approves a gigantic loan bigger than any amount of money you could fathom, and then the individual congressmen take turns standing in the middle of one of those cash grab machines, trying to grab as much of it as they can for their districts and, also, their friends.

In this case, Harry Reid managed to grab $22 million for his friend Robert Bigelow. Now, for those of us who've ever paid for a Subway sandwich with quarters, that may sound like a lot. But I promise you, it isn't. The budget that year was $600 billion. This program got 0.0036666666666666666% of the total budget that year. That's how concerned your government is about aliens.

And yeah, it's probably hard to get government funding for science programs! But for as science-driven as this project claims to be, the paper seems to have had a hell of a time finding even one scientist who didn't get paid to work on the *program who was excited about it. This was about as enthusiastic as any actual scientist got: Still, Mr. Oberg said he welcomed research. "There could well be a pearl there," he said.*

I guess this could technically count as excitement. I mean, this is basically how I react any time they try to re-make Spiderman again. Like, it's not necessary but it's always nice to have the option to watch a new Spiderman, ya know? I just want all the handsome-but-dorky actors in the world to get work, is all.

Now, at this point you might be screaming through tears, "But Anne, what about the billionaire friend of Harry Reid? Surely he made his billions with science and is now doing even more science on top of that!" And ho boy, do I wish that were even partly true.

Robert Bigelow is not a scientist, or an engineer. He's a guy with a Business Administration degree from Arizona State University. Here's how Forbes describes him:

It would be easy to write Robert Bigelow off as an eccentric. He gave $3.7 million to the University of Nevada Las Vegas to establish a "consciousness studies" program that taught classes about life after death. He gave an estimated $10 million to fund the now-defunct UFO-hunting National Institute for Discovery Science. In 1996 he bought a 480-acre Utah cattle ranch that some believe is the site of an interdimensional doorway used by alien shape-shifters and stationed watchers there.

Bigelow's success is evident otherwise. FORBES estimates his real estate empire is worth $700 million. Bigelow is entirely self-made and owns all his companies and properties outright, including the Budget Suites chain of residential *hotels and more than 14,000 apartment and office units across the Southwest.*

You guys, it is easy to write off Robert Bigelow as an eccentric because that is what he is. We have to stop acting like just because someone made a ton of money in real estate between 1970 and 2007 they were some kind of genius. If you were a person with the means to invest in real estate during those years, it'd be more shocking if you didn't make money. Oh, but you want me to give him credit for being "self-made"? Nah:

After earning a business degree from Arizona State University, he returned to Vegas and, with his father's help, started buying, selling, and developing apartment buildings and motels — an easy way to make money in an eternal boomtown. In 1988 he founded Budget Suites of America, an apartment-hotel concept that offered modestly priced, furnished living spaces rentable by the week, month, or year. His timing was perfect: Newcomers in need of comfy but temporary digs were flocking to Las Vegas, Phoenix, and other fast-growing southwestern cities. The privately owned chain now has 18 outlets in three states and has earned him a fortune totaling at least $1 billion (Bigelow declines to comment on his net worth).

Based on this, I can ascertain that Robert Bigelow is a very, very lucky man with a generous father and great timing who is obsessed with space. Good for him. And at least he's passionate about something besides destroying Barack Obama, which is more than I can say for the other guys whose dads set them up with real estate empires during the boom years.

Anyway, aliens. Bigelow believes aliens exist big time, as is his right. And the program he got funding for through his friend and congressman did a lot of work to prove it. Or, well, kinda. What they can tell us they did is interview people who claim to have seen UFOs, and modified some buildings that they claim are being used to house mysterious UFO wreckage. But, of course, that's all according to the guys who are part of the program, so simply taking their word for it only makes sense if you're also still waiting in good faith on a check from an exiled Nigerian prince.

Now, I'll admit, when Mr. Bigelow said Americans are really backwards on the issue of UFOs, my interest was piqued. I do generally believe Americans are really backwards on a lot of things, so could my skepticism be the result of too much mainstream media? Bigelow insists that "China and Russia are much more open and work on this with huge organizations within their countries.

Smaller countries like Belgium, France, England and South American countries like Chile are more open, too." So, I Googled. The most openness I found was in the UK, where they shut down their UFO study program in 2009 and recently released most of the files on it to the public. Among these files is the reasoning behind the program's end:

"No UFO sighting reported to [MoD] has ever revealed anything to suggest an extra-terrestrial presence or military threat to the UK," Carl Mantell of the RAF"s Air Command stated in a briefing to the Defence Minister in 2009. "There is no defence benefit in [MoD] recording, collating, analysing or investigating UFO sightings."

In a way, Bigelow is right, the UK is way more open about how much UFOs have never been proven to exist and are not worth spending tax dollars on. Unless maybe you're a real estate guy who found a way to use government money to renovate your own buildings for "alien stuff storage". Maybe Bigelow is a genius after all.

Now, do I think studying UFOs is inherently bad? No. Do I think aliens are a crazy idea? No. But the existence of this program does not prove that aliens have or are visiting us. What it proves is that Harry Reid wanted to indulge the passion of an "eccentric" billionaire who donated generously to his campaign so he earmarked this money for him as a gesture.

Why am I so mad about this? Because while we're making gestures to rich folk who feel like figuring out if UFOs exist, Maryland is going to have to kick people out of hospitals, Missouri is ending a bunch of currently full medical student training programs, and suburban and rural counties in Illinois are scrambling to figure out how they'll fund their city parks and schools. All of these states are doing this to try and cover budget gaps of $22 million. The exact amount your federal government gave to a guy who was already a billionaire so he could interview some people who saw UFOs. If only the eccentric billionaire campaign contributors of the world could develop obsessions with public health and education.

And yes, all men on the internet, I know that our defense budget doesn't go towards state budgets. But that doesn't make it any more reasonable that our federal government can subsidize a billionaire who wants to go on an alien hunt while the rest of us try to crowd-source public education. If the aliens are visiting us it's no wonder they never stop to chat.

Now, it must be said to unravel the business interests of someone like Robert Bigelow or Brandon Fugal would require substantial investigation. I think it is fair to abide by the old saying of there being no smoke without fire. In Knapp and Kelleher's book published in 2006, mention of the $22 million dollar federal donation is not mentioned. Indeed, they write the below long before the 2017 *New York Times* article revealed the amount given:

In addition, of course, the federal government, which controls the bulk of all science research dollars, frowns upon controversial research projects. Federal funds for research into paranormal topics are all but nonexistent. Small wonder then that so many modern scientists choose to stick with "safe" research projects and goals. The advent of NIDS with comparatively large resources due to the philanthropic generosity of real estate and aerospace entrepreneur Robert Bigelow aimed to at least remove the lack of resources from this part of the equation. However, even with substantial resources, scientists at NIDS still had to face the daunting task of studying something for which very few previous hard data existed...

Knapp, Kelleher, and Bigelow are very slippery characters...

1/ Garth Myers Interviewed by Frank B Salisbury
https://www.theufochronicles.com/2020/04/skinwalker-ranch-original-owner-family-member-speaks.html?m=1

2/ George Knapp
https://en.wikipedia.org/wiki/George_Knapp_(television_journalist)

3/ Linda Moulton Howe
https://en.wikipedia.org/wiki/Linda_Moulton_Howe

4/ Bill Cooper
https://en.wikipedia.org/wiki/Milton_William_Cooper

5/ This Aliens Thing Is A Total Scam
https://medium.com/@annevictoriaclark/this-aliens-things-is-a-total-scam-b82ca9c12a04

SEASON ONE – EPISODE ONE – BAD THINGS HAPPEN WHEN YOU DIG

Narration – *For more than two centuries, a ranch in Utah has been associated with strange and disturbing occurrences that define physical reality. Now, a team of dedicated scientists, researchers, and experts are determined to solve the mystery and reveal the secrets of Skinwalker Ranch.*

The legend is, things happen on this ranch –
Travis Taylor

The series opens with a montage of unexplained phenomena: lights in the sky, cattle mutilations, unexplained knocking from below, and exposure to unknown microwaves...

The screen legend shows:
Skinwalker Ranch Has Been A Center Of UFO And Paranormal Activity For 200 Years.

***

AUGUST 20, 2019, 3:41PM

Dead cow...

High meter readings ...

Travis Taylor, TT, dramatically runs while being filmed...

Someone comments:

Is there really a safe place on this ranch... we're quickly loosing places that are safe to go on this ranch...

The scene then moves to Salt Lake City, Utah...twelve weeks earlier.

***

MAY 28, 2019, 2:53PM

TT aside: *I'm Doctor Travis Taylor, a scientist and physicist*...other aspects of his resume are then given: 25 years or more space and defence industry....NASA... *Dept of Defense and Intelligence Community*...degrees in electrical engineering, aerospace engineering, astronomy, physics, optical sciences...

He describes himself as from Huntsville Alabama, *where rockets that went to the moon were built,* as the team sit round the table...

At this point we know one of either two things about TT: he is an idiot for believing in the moon landing hoax or, and this is more likely, he is an accomplice in the manufacture of this counterfeit universe of television science that is no more than a fairy-tale of the real world.

Brandon Fugal, BF, comes in and shakes hand with TT as others are seated, and he introduces himself as the new owner of Skinwalker Ranch...

BF goes round formally introducing the team to TT:

Erik Bard, EB – Principal Investigator
Jim Segala, JS – Scientist
Thomas Winterton, TW – Ranch Superintendent
Jim Morse, JM – Ranch Manager
Bryant *Dragon* Arnold, BA – Head of Security

BF aside: *I'm Brandon Fugal, the chairman and owner of the largest commercial real estate enterprise here in Utah. I'm also an investor and cofounder of other enterprises involving technology. I grew up middleclass with a very strong religious upbringing. And that upbringing has only helped strengthen my belief that there is more to our existence than meets the eye.*

And I am still looking for the nature of the universe and asking some of these core questions: where did we come from? – why are we here? – where are we going? I truly believe Skinwalker Ranch is a place where some of these questions may be answered or at least better understood.

BF gives the newly formed team a history and geography presentation of the 512 acre ranch:

6:16 – (slide comes up for a fraction of a second.)
Origin of Skinwalker....demonic skinwalker entities...path of the skinwalker...the mesa
1905 – Homesteading commences
1911 – Strange noises
1915 – Indian Tribal Lands . United States Government
1915-1937 – Various Owners – Homesteaders (Locke Family)

BF continues his narration and mentions settlers also seeing unexplained phenomena ...

By 1979 many UFO sightings...

Headlines – September 30, 1976 – *UFO's Cause Stir In Uintah Basin Skies.*

BF reports the hearing of *strange noises* of a hundred years ago or so, along with people *seeing things.* This seems to be the kind of anecdotal evidence that could describe every human habitat on earth over a long enough time period.

BF mentions *acute medical episodes* experienced by people over the years; everything from nausea, perception altering experiences, vertigo, temporary paralysis.

And then the Sherman family acquired the property in 1994. They were witness to some of the most disturbing events on record: cattle mutilations accompanying a twenty five percent decimation of their herd.

BF says that reports from the Sherman family led RB to acquire property *and commence an unprecedented scientific study.*

NIDS transitioned to BASSS and *kept highly confidential ... Many of those professional refuse to step foot on this ranch ever again for the rest of their lives...* [a claim impossible to substantiate and one I doubt.]

At timestamp [7:16] we get BF's slide show:

1996 Robert Bigelow acquires property

1996-2002 – *NIDS Program*

2008 – *BAASS program*

(Side bar National Institute for Discovery Science (NIDS): Privately funded. Staffed (8 fulltime, 5 part time) by PhD/DVM scientists, retired FBI AFOSI investigators and world class

SAB. Utah Ranch was a major focus Sep 1996-2002
[NIDS LOGO]

Bigelow Aerospace Advanced Space Studies (BAASS): Funded by USG. Focus on Advanced Aerospace Technology and Threat Analysis. Staffed (55 full time) by PhD scientists, Engineers, retired military intelligence, law enforcement investigators, Analysts, translators. Utah Ranch focus Nov-2011/2012

[BIGELOW AEROSPACE LOGO])

In 2016 I purchased Skinwalker Ranch and assembled our team to carry through this investigation forward into the next level...

***

Questions that might occur to the reader of *Th€ Cur$€ of $kinwa£k€r Ranch:*

What can a real estate guy discover that the unlimited resources of the federal government can't?

Did RB discover anything, and if so, where's the proof?

What was RB really up to?

Why did RB eventually sell the ranch to BF?

***

BF refers to Erik Bard and the monitoring equipment, and continues to narrate:

One of the first thing we captured was a 500 ft section of the mesa became totally illuminated...

[IMAGES CAPTURED JANUARY 19, 2018 1:41 AM]
Column of light above mesa
[VIDEO RECORDED DECEMBER 23, 2018 5:52 PM]
Picture of UFO
[VIDEO RECORDED DECEMBER 23, 2017 4:42 AM]

There is speculation among the team that the ranch will *misbehave* when TT shows up. The ranch apparently *reacts* to new people – or is it because the *documentary* is being filmed?

***

MAY 29, 2019, 10:27 AM

10:20 BF and TT talk in car...

BF says to TT, *welcome to Aerodynamic.*

They transfer from sportscar to helicopter after being introduced to Cameron and Matthew Fugal. TTs piloted by Cameron. Cameron gives a short prayer...

Is this genuine piety or fake piety?

When first witnessing what I later regarded as rank hypocrisy, I later reflected that these Mormons lying to the general public for the good of the Utah economy might be how they justify their *spirituality.*

MAY 29, 2019 11:30 AM

They approach the ranch. CF flys TT near mesa, *but not over it* because of *warnings,* and so emphasising the bugaboo nature of the ranch...

TT is greeted by team when the chopper lands...

Bearing in mind that at the end of series two when TT leaves the ranch in his red car like a cowboy riding into the sunset, it is likely that TT may have already arrived at the ranch by car and subsequently given a helicopter tour of the ranch rather than arrived at by air. Like certain scripting elements, one always needs to ask a rather open ended question:

In a supposedly scientific documentary series, where does artistic licence end and deception begin?

EB shows TT the inner sanctum, observation system, *Sentinel Assignment Telemetry And Notification S.A.T.A.N I wonder how this invocation of SATAN — surely an acronym that was sought — sits with CF's helicopter prayer?*

***

MAY 29, 2019 12:27 PM

They ride towards mesa and stop off at the livestock former holding area.

BF aside: He mentions the Sherman family experiencing UFO sightings and cattle mutilations...

At timestamp [20:53], a newspaper clipping 1956-1973 UFO sighting...1996 caption: *Rancher Terry Sherman stands on his ranch near one of the soil impressions, which has faded with time...*

The *Shermans* seem like a plot device as much as a real family. We do not hear from them directly, but always from proxies who knew them, and allege many things on their behalf.

BF aside: *I don't blame them for selling the property. They were terrorised...*

Back at the livestock area...

TT is told of large wolf by JS

JS: He describes how the wolf gets shot many times and seemed miraculously nonplussed by it all. This account is given in *The Hunt For The Skinwalker*. So JS is merely repeating Skinwalker Ranch *canon.*

JM aside: He speaks about the Utes and the Navaho crossing each other... Utes were using the Navaho as slaves. The Navaho's cursed this land, *which is now in the path of the skinwalker*; a shapeshifting spirit.

After they arrive and go up the mesa TT shows his TriField meter to the camera. It displays

10.869 mW/m² . He had previously explained how these instruments can measure static electrical fields, magnetic field, and radiofrequencies – and it was on this last setting that the milliwatts per metre squared reading was taken.

The intrepid reader may also like to consider whether some of the one star reviews on Amazon may suggest the reason for the TriField meter — a propriety brand after all said and done — is featured to the degree it is.

One apparently knowledgeable if ungrammatical three star reviewer said of the TriField TF2 meter:[1]

after almost a year of research and learning exactly how to measure and fix issues of RF radiation this meter doesn't work. some of the top experts with EMF mitigation all agree you can trust this meter with the mag readings. But the RF and electrical readings aren't accurate. If your serious and need a trusted meter for RF readings use the safe and sound pro ii...

TT aside: *We found electromagnetic radiation that shouldn't be there at dangerous levels that could be harmful to humans...*

TT suggests it was coming from different directions and mentions it being stronger than from Wi-Fi or a cell phone and says:

Microwaves like that just don't exist in nature. So where was this microwave radiation coming from?

When I originally started making notes on the series I found it amazing that TT doesn't mention microwave weapons – even though his biography says he's worked with direct energy weapons. Microwave weapons aren't even mentioned in order to rule them out.

Indeed, I reflected:

Is this man with umpteen degrees naïve enough to believe the moon landings as well as not being targeted, or just an actor?

With the progression of time I realised it was so much easier to have a team of actors who simply told lies about instrumentation than having men in black hiding in the bushes with electromagnetic weaponry. And of course, some jiggery-pokery with other gadgets to spike meter readings wouldn't be ruled out either in order to get instruments to go haywire for the cameras.

And speaking of the cameras...and as countless critical observers have noticed, *how come the cameras that film the show never malfunction?*

The show's powers that be actually say there were malfunctioning cameras, but only after many made the initial observation. The useful idiot fandom in Facebook groups of course repeat the fiction of the cameras going wrong.

***

MAY 29, 2019 1:16 PM

They drive back to the Command Center...

TT suggests measuring with *fifty TriField meters all the time,* plus a complete radiation sweep...

I wonder what became of this suggestion – down the memory hole of course.

The ranch is mentioned as being downwind from *nuclear tests.* A headline, *Terrific Atom Blast Rocks South Nevada* a few hundred mile to the west is highlighted. TT speculates on radioactive fallout as being a cause for various phenomena.

TT describes digging holes then they discuss digging; the team *don't like it.*

BA: *that's the trigger ...when you dig, bad stuff happen...*

And so, one of the show's favourite plot devices is thus born.

TW aside: he describes a *big goose egg on the back of his head* after digging.

I originally entertained the idea that TW was a witless dupe of microwave weaponry. Now I believe the bandage, the tubing about the face, and the look of dejection were all hoaxed. In the month of April 2019 I had been in hospital myself for a minor operation. The thought of taking a selfie would have struck me as absurd.

Now, I'm not enamoured of TW to the degree his female groupies are, and for his sake I hope this photo is playacting for the sake of the overall grift and scam rather than an example of supreme narcissism.

1/ Amazon Review of TriField TF2 meter
https://www.amazon.com/product-reviews/B078T2R64C/ref=acr_dp_hist_3?ie=UTF8&filterByStar=three_star&reviewerType=all_reviews#reviews-filter-bar

SEASON ONE – EPISODE TWO – NIGHT VISIONS

Peril strikes during a daring investigation as the team embarks on their quest to understand what may lie beneath Skinwalker Ranch.

***

A big *neodymium* magnet is brought out. They continue their round table discussion from the Command Center...

TT: *What does this have to do with not digging on the ranch?*

The magnet supposedly reproduces the effect EB obtained on a still shot of the mesa...

TT aside: *Does he think there's some giant magnet buried under the ground that's causing some of these strange phenomena?*

EB reiterates ideas about some magnetic field generating machines above or below...

The team decide to carry on *gathering evidence...*

***

MAY 30, 2019 9:41 AM

TT aside: He mentions two teams of outside contractors will look for dangerous levels radiation, including microwaves...

They travel to *Homestead Two*.

TW aside: He describes seeing *shadow figures*, hearing voices on multiple occasions – just like the Shermans. These voices are supposedly corroborated by others. They tell him, *to stop what he was doing or to leave*...

Curiously, this observation of TW's is never visited again in the series as far as I am aware. If I'd witnessed this, I'm sure I'd mention it every episode. TW also describes the relationship of Utes and Navaho: The Utes joined up with the White man and were subsequently cursed by the Navaho etc.

MAY 30, 2019 9:53 AM

TT and TW while travelling in the car are called over to the cave-sink hole on the mesa. They are above and not far from Homestead Two. People in the hole allegedly experience vertigo and nausea...

Jeff Fitzmayer, JF, from *Semper Environmental* is measuring radio wave frequencies while Travis Snowder, TS, and Casey Smith from *Qal-Tek Associates*, are doing full radiation sweeps...

They are also looking for VOCs — Volatile Organic Compounds — and other chemicals.

TS: reports VOC levels of 3600 parts per billion; a high abnormality and dangerous level is thereby suggested.

TT faulters, and reports he doesn't feel very

well and has difficulty in holding his balance. He reports that his knees are feeling shaky; he feels as though that he hasn't eaten and then worked out; that he feels like there is low blood sugar levels and is having trouble breathing. No others feel similar. And incidents of lone individuals not feeling well rather than groups of people in toto are to be the exclusive provenance of Skinwalker Ranch in future episodes. Of the shows' regulars, it is TT and TW — *the best actors?* — who *suffer* from the *phenomenon*.

Originally I had not ruled out the targeting of individuals, but I do now after reviewing the whole Skinwalker production. TT is lying or acting – it depends on your perspective.

TTs battery went dead on his phone – as allegedly did CS's phone...

CS hands out dosimeters and there is discussion of Homestead Two.

BF aside: He mentions buying the ranch off aerospace and real estate guy Robert Bigelow. He reports that RB and his team experienced the full gamut of unexplained phenomena:

Most of what Mr Bigelow and his team studied and reported on the ranch remains either classified or confidential, and he's walked away..

The team setup prior to nightfall: camera, telescopes etc

***

NIGHT MAY 31, 2019

They shine laser on mesa and view with infra-red camera. A significant part of this episode to deconstruct is the alleged anomalous laser behaviour. That is when another *mystery* beam seems to accompany the main beam. This is in fact due to an internal reflection, and is one of many pieces of information I am indebted to Royce L Robertson for bringing to my attention.[1]

As significant as the Skinwalker team of experts' apparent ignorance — *including TT's PhD in optical science* — is the shows' producers running with complete disinformation. Perhaps they should consult the book, *Introduction to Laser Science and Engineering*... ?

But ...oh...the author is TT...who lists a PhD in optical science among his wallpaper collection...

The team climb up the mesa, and the following aside is given:

IMAGES CAPTURED JANUARY 19, 2018 1:41 AM showing laser and illuminations from around it...

VIDEO RECORDED DECEMBER 23, 2018 5:52 PM light coming up *from the* mesa...

For what it's worth, it seems to me to originating from *behind* it...

They film and report on a *strange glow*...where TT reports this isn't a hoax or special effect as he may possibly have previously possibly surmised... But why haven't they put cameras on top of mesa? Or at least closer?

MAY 31, 2019 4:38 AM

They see a beam of light coming up from the ground.

JS oversees an aluminum foil directional finder in one plane to try and attempt to see if there is a direction to any radiofrequencies. It affirms the direction of the mesa.

TT: *There is something here, on this ranch that is broadcasting microwaves and at times reach powers like a microwave oven.*

JS...*And it's not Wi-Fi, it's not cell phones...*
Just then TW reports he doesn't feel well...
He's taken to hospital...

***

COMMAND CENTER MAY 31, 2019 5:54 AM

BF is called by BA who reports the TW incident...

BA: *I'm armed to the teeth and feel like I might as well be carrying a fly swatter...*

This is as dramatic as it is a non-sequitur – just like the neodymium magnet prop at the start of the episode.

When did guns ever give protection against the supposed supernatural?

1/ Internal Reflections
https://www.youtube.com/watch?v=x79SlmMNI5U

SEASON ONE – EPISODE THREE – LOOKING DOWN

A life-threatening incident forces the team to re-assess their methods of investigation, and disturbing new evidence at homestead one has Tom and Travis on edge.

***

There is phone conversation between BA and BF about TW. On the next take, they are all gathered around the table...

A CT scan of TW *seems to show a lump in the same place as two years previously.* No protuberance of TW's head is that evident however.

BA reports high readings on the radiofrequency scale prior to incident.

TW is welcomed back to the ranch...

JS aside: *His injuries were consistent with a radiation beam that entered his body from a specific angle, an angle of attack back behind his head.*

JS then shows diagram of beam going into head. Top/back of head. Once again, JS is a university PhD. Why doesn't he even mention the possibility of a microwave targeting by the military industrial complex? I mean, they could simply mention it and then rule it out because of surveillance, couldn't they?

That JS refrained from further filming after series one indicates to me that he had had enough of the farce, and he may have felt his reputation is worth more than what he was being paid.

***

COMMAND CENTER
JUNE 2, 2019, 3:38 PM

BF convenes a round table meeting and asks whether they should go ahead.

BF gives out wearable censor devices that are radiation and *stress measurer watches*.

We are given momentary view of the helicopter through a window with a grey alien logo. In fact, this iconography occurs in many place over the ranch. Everyone is free to decorate as they wish, but this indicates to me that it's all about *television science* rather than *real science*. It is also conditioning viewers on a near subliminal level to accept exotic explanations for ranch *events*.

***

JUNE 4, 2019, 7.55 AM

TT aside: He mentions that it *doesn't add up* that despite their non-invasive investigation TW still suffered...

Derrick Ward, DW, owner of *Hot Shots Aerial Photography* is introduced to the team. He uses thermal imaging among his $35,000 equipment.

EB aside: He speaks about Robert Bigelow's findings never being fully released. *Rumours of some kind of base or an alien artefact beneath the property*. He is hopeful that a drone can show some sort of imagery...

Perhaps the simplest answer is that RB actually discovered nothing. That he may have been engaged in other government funded work, or was merely the recipient of ill-judged and misdirected tax payer money, is something else altogether.

The drone takes off, and they look at the thermal imaging.

BF aside: He describes how immediately on RB occupation, watchtowers and razor wire were installed. Livestock were placed in enclosures and observation was enabled. *The findings*, we are told, *remain under lock and key...*

Nothing is seen by the drone, and the drone is then taken over to Homestead Two. This was built in 1905 and not lived in since the 1930s. Once again, Appendix A will help the reader get a bearing on Skinwalker Ranch landmarks.

BA aside: He reckons a lot of the strangeness centres around the homesteads. He recalls batteries going down to zero in a matter of seconds, people feeling vertigo, or even *not being able to hear sound.*

HOMESTEAD TWO
JUNE 4, 2019, 8:26 AM

A drone prepares to take off but *no connection* between itself and the control unit is forthcoming.

TT aside: With respect to battery draining, he says, *we can't figure out why...*

Perhaps they should use the same batteries the cameras use?

Once again, malicious human use of

microwaves is something I eventually ruled out, but why don't this team of *experts* at least consider this if they are genuine researchers?

EB picks up a 5 GHz signal. They then pack it up for the day.

At this point it must be observed that drones are subsequently used on a frequent basis without them breaking down. Further, as well as being used by the investigation team, they are used to film diverse shots such as the helicopter from above when its landed, and the porch area when the team have congregated there.

The mysterious skinwalker phenomenon therefore seems to be in sync with the need to have a week by week mystery. Is as though the *phenomenon* — to objectify it — has decided that it can't be bothered to interfere with drones after week three. Perhaps the *phenomenon* realises it needs to *play up* on a novel week by week basis?

Meanwhile TT oversees putting meters in coffee cans in order to filter out the extraneous directions from which they will be pointed towards.

8:45 PM

They arrange a triangulation using angles of elevation and conclude that the source is a 5700 ft ~ 1900 yards ~ mile up. Whether the measurement is accurate, is moot.

TT aside: He believes what causes this should be seen by the naked eye, and once again says, *this just doesn't add up...*

Not for the first time, TT sound like a leading scientist in a sci fi B film.

***

THREE DAYS LATER
JUNE 7, 2019, 12:21 PM

They try weather balloons, calling in Matt Turner, MT, PhD engineer, from the University of Alabama, Huntsville...

At the triangulation point near the mesa, a balloon has been equipped with a compass, camera, and tri meter... JS looks sceptical.

Back at the control room, the telemetry stops. It's at ~10,500 ft and not updating...

MT is baffled and says the censor is rock-solid; he's done it over thirty times, *it's never failed on me.*

The height is reckoned to be the same as before after the height above sea level is taken into account.

They look at footage from the recovered camera as it was directed at the meter. It showed 0.3 mW/m^2 and according to TT that is, *like standing next to a microwave oven.*

MT ask TT whether this is someone just sending a Wi-Fi signal back and forth, but TT discounts this.

JS mentions *it must come from off planet* because of the increase (RF energy / frequency) at higher altitude.

Off planet feeds into the steering towards the ET answer; satellite is not mentioned, yet isn't this an obvious avenue of exploration? No human agency for extraneous radiation is ever explored by the Skinwalker *experts.*

***

HOMESTEAD ONE
JUNE 8, 2019, 11:46 AM

Strange noises have been heard in the cellar by the caretakers Kandus Linde, KL, and Tom Lewis, TL. They have only been on the ranch a few weeks.

TW aside: He mentions that the ranch has had three sets of ownership before BF took it over. Of the previous occupants, we hear: the Myers reported strange rumblings; the Shermans reported groceries coming out plus other weird anomalies; and RB took on the ranch in 1996. Once again TW is just repeating Skinwalker canon.

TW describes drilling through into the source of these strange noises brought to his attention by KL and TL. They subsequently observe small animal bones and the possible remains of a small fire – quite an anti-climax...

SEASON ONE – EPISODE FOUR – HIGH STRANGENESS

It's an historic moment when the entire team witnesses, and documents, two UFO sightings directly over Skinwalker Ranch.

***

HOMESTEAD ONE
JUNE 8, 2019, 12:14 PM

In Homestead One, occupied by the caretakers TL and KL, the team knock down a wall in the basement. Both we are told knew BF from a young age. TL worked in IT. KL is a published anthropologist, and has co-authored the *Atlas of Human Cranial Macromorphoscopic Traits*. More on the caretakers in Appendix B.

KL and TL had previously heard *strange noises*. The enclosed room with no apparent outlets gives up a few small animal bones. They make a big deal about why the room was there and sealed off.

TL aside: He reports they've *heard some strange things...strange noises from the basement, strange vibrations coming from the ground...*

On first watching this episode I speculated this was either a fabrication or there is a need for physical explanation. When you come around to believing everyone is lying or grossly exaggerating, the need for multifarious explanations is reduced to one.

TL recalls strange things experienced by the Shermans...

TT speculates, *but how could anything get inside a completely sealed up concrete room ...*

The team adjourn to the Command Center and discuss findings. They look under a microscope at the bone fragments. They decide it is bone – shock horror. TT leads the discussion; KL is the anthropologist but seems subdued by *Mr Know-It-All*, TT. The crushed up bones are both a mystery and as anti-climatic as a Dave Allen joke.[1]

***

Cattle are brought in as biosensors...

BF asserts that cattle mutilations going back to the 1930s have occurred. I have seen no proof of this. I do concede that cattle mutilations have taken place in modern times, and usually in American states. Now, if you are like me, you will not believe the mutilation phenomena are of extraterrestrial origin.

The psyop of inferring ET culpability is one that Linda Moulton Howe has built her UFO career on; a career that has seen her become a narcisstic cats paw for intelligence agencies. Suffice to say, I go over much of this in my book, *Fake Aliens And The Phony Nuke World Order*.

BF aside: He mentions bait pens and observation towers after RB took over. This is when it first occurred to me that maybe RB was involved in performing cattle mutilations.

BF: He says most of what RB and team discovered *remains classified or confidential and is locked away...*

COMMAND CENTER
JUNE 15, 2019

The team are preparing rockets...

TT aside: He gives a recap of the balloons' instrumentation: RF sensors, a spectrum analyser, and a gamma ray detector.

They are now set to repeat the balloon experiment but with rockets.

JS reports cows huddling together. In fact the cattle *behaving strangely* is a recurring theme. Cattle can huddle or stampede for fear of predators are when chasing newly deposited cut grass for example.

The first rocket crashes and the parachute doesn't open.

TT aside: The electromagnetic spectrum showing RF through microwaves, visible light, UV, and gamma rays is scrutinised.

Meanwhile, the cows start to congregate.

***

At timestamp [23:23] a UFO is claimed to be seen.

At the time I wondered whether some sort of drone synchronisation with a Skinwalker Ranch *insider* facilitated this. Now, I wonder whether this was just video trickery *after the fact*. This should be discerned as the easiest way of doing it once one realises that everyone is in on the Skinwalker fraud. I ask forbearance on the part of the reader on this matter.

The truth is, most of the time, most people are truthful towards us. It is a shock to the system to realise the wealthy are not only psychopaths, but this psychopathy is often the reason for the most significant monetary difference between the *haves* and most of us, the *have-nots*.

The second rocket is successful

BF aside : He describes the film footage as *nothing short of historic*. But why not just ascribe it as *historic*? Why the need to embellish with *nothing short of*?

TT aside: He describes thinking previous accounts of UFOs were products of *overactive imagination...I never thought I see one in person...*

This is just BS. He must know that UFOs exist. It's their interpretation that is contentious. Indeed, he is well aware of the famous US Navy *Tic Tac* footage. Bearing in mind he's appearing in a documentary series that occurs on a channel that shows UFOs for breakfast, lunch, and dinner, the assertion that he never thought he'd see one in person is pure nonsense.

EB aside: He says he wants to examine it frame by frame ...

TT aside: He speculates whether the rocket caused the UFO to appear and become visible or whether it was a coincidence because they were looking up.

As they are preparing third rocket, a UFO appears again; still in the same spot, it is visible and then invisible in a cloudless sky.

During preparation BA doesn't feel so well...

BF aside: The fact that the entire team saw this; this changes our whole investigation at Skinwalker Ranch.

I have since doubted this observation, and suggest after the fact photoshopping. Further, applying statement analysis to BF saying the entire team saw this seems redundant if true and therefore suspicious because we can clearly see the whole team making a song and a dance about a probable clear sky, secure in the knowledge that *Photoshop* can cast its spell on the show's cult followers.

***

JUNE 15, 2019, 7:14 PM

TT aside: He links BA being unwell to the UFO. TT recalls his own queasy feelings and TW's hospitalisation. He observes that some intense RF radiation is apparently coming from above the ranch...

After the third launch they go to the Command Center to look at surveillance film. They also look at Geiger counter hits. There are more at the rocket's apogee, and so they link them to the UFO.

TT aside : *I don't believe in UFOs period...*

What an asinine statement. Any flying object not identified is a *UFO* by definition. If this statement reflected his disbelief in ET visitation, he must surely have to attribute the RF and gamma readings as being of human origin...

EB reminds them they must contact BF. BF too speculates on the tests causing the UFO to manifest.

BF aside: He describes seeing a UFO, *a few years ago*, above the mesa.

BA aside: He comments that after many years at ranch, he sees his first UFO.

At timestamp [40 minutes], a montage of UFO imagery from 2017 and 2018 is shown.

BF aside: *Are we alone? Do we live in a multidimensional universe? Are we being visited or are we being interacted with? Skinwalker Ranch, I believe, is an incredible living laboratory or a place where some of these questions may be answered or at least better understood...*

1/ Dave Allen Ghost Story

https://www.youtube.com/watch?v=G_GA88xBgAk

SEASON ONE – EPISODE FIVE – DANGEROUS CURVES

When advanced testing shows evidence of strange anomalies under the ranch, Brandon finally gives the team permission to dig.

***

    TT has his own trailer on Skinwalker Ranch; just like a *film star* and clearly the role designated for him. He was brought in to join a supporting cast and become the hero of this fake made-for-TV investigation. His Wikipedia biography is almost unbelievable. It reads like a boy's own action hero. Factor in his *man of the people* persona, exemplified by his unabashed Alabama accent, and any criticism of TT might seem to be beyond the pale of polite discourse. I however, do go beyond the pale. TT is a one man BS factory.

    It should be noted that TT is one of the few Skinwalker Ranch team with a Wikipedia biography. He seems more likely a Hollywood creation than a real man. In addition to this show he has authored and co-authored numerous books. When I first encountered *The Curse Of Skinwalker Ranch* the man behind the persona of TT became a burning question to me. The profundity of TT resides in the sheer depth of his shallowness.

***

William the dog wakes TT up at 4.51 AM. We hear but don't see him. There's a camera outside trailer to record him going outside in response. TT goes and checks on the spectrum analyser. The signal is oscillating between 26MHz and 2GHz

TT: *I've never seen anything like it in my life...*

I'm sure exclamations of this kind by TT could be turned into a drinking game...

COMMAND CENTER
8:47 AM

TT reports strange noise from distance and sees a range of frequencies from microwave band down to hand bands of 35Mhz.

TT doesn't know *how you could do that...*

TT aside: He reviews strange things happening since he's been there.

TT rotates a chalkboard to reveal a picture of wormhole and invokes Einstein as a possible explanation. JS nods in approval. BA visibly (acting?) shows confusion and disbelief. He looks like he might have been told to show a look of bemusement. The gaze he makes becomes iconic for him and the subject of many memes.

TT asserts wormholes while being theoretical, can be the only thing to explain what happening over here. That has to be one of the biggest cartloads of BS to have been uttered on the show so far.

TT moves from this to suggesting a lens like function is being carried out by the 70 mile terrain, focusing energy to the point — a mile up or so — where it is alleged to be.

TT invokes Einstein and sci fi movies. JS jumps in and adds a little bit of mumbo jumbo. And BA carries on an episode by episode refinement of his *redneck bemusement* look...

At this point I want to declare that this is not only the stuff of straight up science fiction, but the whole spacetime paradigm of cosmology attributed to Albert Einstein has been receiving some serious criticism from *Electric Universe Theory,* EUT. In my humble opinion EUT will eventually replace *Special* and *General Relativity.*

More on this can be found on the *Thunderbolts YouTube* channel. However, it is unnecessary to disbelieve in Einstein's theories to realise the TV show is bogus. I just give my opinion on this for folk interested in the more theoretical aspects of physics. Once again, TT's large collection of paper certificates are, I submit, indicative of stupidity rather than genuine scientific ability.

BF aside: He discusses RB again. Recounts stories about portals opening at Homestead Two: *other landscapes they can see through these portals...that are difficult to describe...*

But why would the government allow private individuals potential access to these portals?

TT at the chalk board mentions the *wormhole hypothesis is* the *only one that fits,* they should collect ground penetrating radar, and make resistivity measurements. TT is absolutely full of it.

JULY 1, 2019, 10:18 AM

Phillip Oviatt, PO, and Zachary Zyla, ZZ, as Ground Penetrating Radar, GPR, experts are introduced.

TT asks them to map out the roads.

TT aside: He describes two methods: ground penetrating radar works by sending radio waves into ground and measuring reflection. And soil resistivity uses metal stakes and wires to sound a current into the ground.

EB aside: He mentions less invasive methods – not digging – should be preferred.

They discover the batteries on the GPRs are very low. The implication of course is that an unnatural discharge has taken place.

The Skinwalker *phenomenon* will again strike against any novel equipment when initially deployed, but it will *thoughtfully neglect* to do so with equipment it has already interfered with.

EB aside: He reviews the various phenomena.

Two teams now proceed with parallel commentary. One GPR is dragged behind a vehicle; however, just before they set off, a security guard shows his mobile phone is playing up.

EB and team run the GPR from the Command Center along ranch road to the old Homestead Two. He suggests anomalies could be utilities.

PO points out *domes anomalies*. He mentions a *possible tunnel*, and a *metal structure – could it be a utility pipe?* This occurs in the same area as where the drone was previously faulty – what a surprise (not).

JULY 1, 2019, 10:25 AM

TT takes ZZ and TW to a field to do resistivity testing. TT vaguely mentions *myths and stories*. They receive a call from EB and join up at Homestead Two bringing the resistivity equipment with them.

HOMESTEAD TWO
12:.05 PM

PO mentions they have found a *parallel structure* at Homestead Two.

JS speculates underground features causing above ground phenomena to occur.

They run GPR at Homestead Two while EB and his team take resistivity readings up on the mesa.

GPR finds a structure on the same line as the well/cistern.

TT lifts a well cover despite an injunction not to do from JS.

Let's reminds ourselves that both JS and TT are alleged "men of science"

BF aside: He recounts the catatonic trance of someone upright and in trance, near the same feature. Of course, we only have his word for it.

TT doesn't feel too well after lifting. A high dosemeter reading — of ionising radiation, 120 m rad /sec , beeping, *pretty high* — is claimed. As far as we know, as usual, the skinwalker phenomenon is careful not to do anything to the cameramen – how considerate of it/he/she...

TT aside: He says of the radiation, *equivalent to 20,000 full body x -ray scan at an airport... five times more than the legal limit allows in a year.* He is allegedly diagnosed later with radiation burns.

TT's dosimeter is higher than JS's.

JS: Speaking of the radiation, *you're not going to see it in the middle of nowhere, guaranteed...*

TT decides they should stop what they're doing and leave...

So, why weren't previous folk around Homestead Two ever diagnosed with radiation burns I wonder?

TT aside: He goes to the doctor with red marks on hands and head. The implied gamma radiation could be insect bites or even makeup. This exposure to gamma radiation if genuine should have at least invited the possibility of some nefarious human agency before invoking the supernatural. Of course it didn't, and this in itself suggests more BS from TT and the team.

***

TWO DAYS LATER
COMMAND CENTER
JULY 3, 2019, 1:12 PM

There is a discussion of the data collected...

PO is concentrating on Homestead Two.

TT takes it up and without pausing for thought draws a rugby ball shaped saucer object underground.

This thing is a thousand ft long, he opines...

Everything on Skinwalker Ranch is not made of elements from the periodic table as far as TT is concerned, it is entirely made up of the elements hyperboleum and BS.

But why doesn't PO, the GPR expert articulate this point of view about the supposed underground object? Although he later just calls it an *anomalous area*, TT is again away with the fairies describing something akin to *Quatermass And The Pit* that of course featured a buried space vehicle. I can imagine the snack watching cult followers getting well off on this narrative, and of course this is why *Prometheus* through TT with the help of the other players feeds this narrative.

TT aside: He says, *it looks like a two story facility ... We have a thousand foot long oval shaped object that appears to be buried underground at Homestead Two. Now, this is the same place where a lot of bizarre happenings...even UFO siting have been reported over the years, so the question is: are they related?*

TT mentions he would like to dig there. BA is against it. BA and TT call BF from trailer and speak about taking core samples. BA previously expresses concern that he hasn't a PhD, so *his opinion doesn't count.* This is soap opera gold. Fans of the show often say they can't understand why BA has such a say in things when the scientific *experts* should be calling the shots. The simple answer is that BA's inertia is something that needs to be scripted in order for the soap opera drama and suspense to persist. Their criticism is like fans of *Dallas* saying the programme would be better without JR or that *Batman* could exist in a comic book universe without super villains.

TT mentions on the phone to BF *that if there is any place on the ranch where X marks the spot, it's right there in the middle of the road, right in front of Homestead Two.*

They come to a compromise on core drilling. And of course this initiates a plot device that we'll see time and time again...

SEASON ONE – EPISODE SIX – POKING THE NEST

When advanced testing shows evidence of strange anomalies under the ranch, Brandon finally gives the team permission to dig.

***

JULY 23, 2019, 1: 13 PM

The fitting of more surveillance cameras takes place.

TL aside: He speaks of cattle mutilations.

KL and TL report back to EB about the bunching up of cattle and mention the benefits of cameras...

***

TWO DAYS LATER
JULY 25, 2019, 9:07 AM

TT aside: He describes another sweep of the area for radiation before core drilling takes place...

BF aside: He speaks of the hesitancy in giving the go ahead for any digging as we see *Qal-Tek*

Associates turn up at the ranch. They are equipped with radiation detectors. Casey Smith, CS, also shows up. TT briefs him on previous radiation incidents.

At Homestead Two, TT gives a brief aside about letting CS *figure out* what's going on over there. And here I had to reflect again on TT's alleged radiation burns. If they weren't of paranormal origin but real, where is the need to eliminate some human agency? Since there isn't, and even if supernatural forces were regarded as being culpable, then surely the scientific method would be invoked to eliminate probable causes. The absence of any attempt to eliminate human agency demonstrates the complete Skinwalker BS operation.

Gamma radiation isn't identified on any regular basis from now on in the Skinwalker franchise, and on this occasion they just find nothing more than *background radiation* all around – even by the well.

***

JULY 26, 2019, 7:33 AM

TT aside: He notes that alpacas are being delivered to see if exotic animals trigger any strange phenomena.

KL and TL aside: Accompanying the alpaca unloading as we watch, they speak of the *mystery* of the ranch; notwithstanding, they say people *think they are crazy* for wanting to be there...

I would like to know of the people who do think they are crazy. As a cynic I see them getting paid. Skinwalker fandom is jealous of not being able to live on the ranch. I have difficulty being able to identify a demographic who would describe them as *crazy*.

LATER THAT DAY
COMMAND CENTER
2.24 PM

TT, BA, and TW are introduced by JM to Larry Cesspooch, LC, a Ute *Spiritual Leader*.

TT aside: *speaks as* a *scientist*, he is nevertheless *open to paranormal phenomena..*

LC speaks of the area as a funnel, seemingly and conveniently, corroborating TT's wormhole diagrams. He continues to describe that a lot of people have called it a portal...*something not of this earth*...he goes on to describe the *skinwalker* and Ute language term....coyote like...*things come at night...*

There are suspenseful audio beats as cameras pick up dramatic head turns. Reality TV producers are fond of filming these gyrations.

BF aside: He describes the curse between the Navaho and Ute tribes. The Ute were aligned with the US government and sold the Navaho into slavery. The Navaho we are told, cursed the land:

The Skinwalker is essentially a witch that has chosen to put on the skin essentially, or the form of what can only be described as a giant wolf. A skinwalker is something that exhibits super human agility and strength. Placing the skinwalker curse on this property made it a very real place to avoid.

LC has spoken of a ritual to prevent harm for the curse that they engage with.

TT aside : *Who knows, perhaps it will help to keep us safe...*

BA takes his hat off as a display of reverence as LC begins his ritual:

Look, Father, Creator of all good things, this land. Ute people...let me hear you. Help these men who... want to know what it is. Help us. [he spreads tobacco on road]. *Help us* [he spreads more tobacco on road]. *Thank you, Creator. Good Spirits.*

LC warns that if anything happens then they should stop what they are doing...

***

HOMESTEAD TWO
JULY 27, 2019, 10:07 AM

BA aside: As the drill rig pulls up, he speaks of disquiet about disturbing the earth...

TT aside: He reminds us of the anomaly discovered by GPR. But the only thing to do is to dig a hole.

10:26 AM

Snowshoe Engineering: Jeremy LeBeau, JL, Benjamin Laidlow, BL, and Warren White, WW, are briefed by TT in the presence of CS.

TW aside: He testifies that he believes in a paranormal influence based on his own experiences.

CS checks for radioactive material in shallow core samples, but there is nothing there...

CURRENT DEPTH: 14 FT

TARGET DEPTH 15-20 FT

Still no radioactive material...

At 17 ft something hard is struck...

TT aside: He speculates about alien object underneath...

They move closer to Homestead Two and BA expresses disquiet again.

The team observe the power line overhead is wobbling prior to the next planned drilling.

TT says, *it's crazy*, and in an aside describes the event, *as being like an earthquake.*

But the ground is not said to be moving.

So, one explanation is that someone is using a device to shake the telegraph poles a little way off? Or could it be as simple as the camera being deliberately shaken?

BA and EB do a radiation sweep of Homestead Two.

TT asks BA about how he feels...

BA aside: He describes the delayed reaction of things happening on the ranch. This *delayed reaction* idea seems to be another device to circumscribe real science with drama by removing the immediacy of one event following another concomitant with the idea of causality. One of the simplest codifications of this principle is *Newton's Third Law of Motion*:

To very action there is an equal and opposite reaction.

The absurdity of negating causality is often seen in cartoons and slapstick where Wile E. Coyote is *treading air* after running off a cliff and the realisation precedes gravity, or a comedy actor is hit on the head with a frying pan and says *ouch* ten seconds later.

***

COMMAND CENTER
JULY 28, 2019, 7:02 AM

There are signs of distress among the alpacas, taken from the video of the unmanned display devices in EB's operations base.

8:07 AM

Dr Nelson Duncan, ND, is greeted by Kaleb Bench, KB, security.

TL aside: He mentions waking up to a

screaming sound he wasn't familiar with...

There is a video of injury to one alpaca from. But from wolves or mountain lions perhaps?

ND mentions as he sutures the wound that previous owners went away because they were a little scared. This attack from a wild animal is then conflated in the people's minds by TL's mention of cattle mutilations. TL asks ND what he remembers. ND then relates one experience he remembers.

BF aside: He recalls how the Sherman family brought the ranch the in the early 90s and experienced everything from UFOs to *countless cattle mutilations*. This is standard BF hyperbole, there were many mutilations, but they weren't countless. His recollection is accompanied by the newspaper headline:[1]

Utah rancher claims UFO sightings, cattle mutilations, crop circles July 5, 1996.

Interestingly, the crop circles are the *original type;* that is, concomitant with circular craft landing. There is every reason to believe the original reported crop circles were landing impressions from circular antigravity flying machines. I describe this in *Fake Aliens And The Phony Nuke World Order*. The various complex designs often appearing in Wiltshire, England, have been created by hoaxers.

BF conflates the skinwalker with UFO activity again, as motivation for the Shermans to sell the ranch.

The scene now goes back to the corral where the alpacas are kept and ND as finished suturing the wound animal. Clearly we are led to wonder whether this is the work of the skinwalker.

***

COMMAND CENTER
JULY 28, 2019 10:48 AM

TL describes a *big dog* – contradicted by KL. While the camera focuses on BA, he gives a look of horror and *told you so*.

BA describes the camera *going down* – how convenient. But the camera from TT's trailer is able to pick up alpaca's being alarmed. I suspect they caught a natural predator attacking the alpacas and then improvised a skinwalker inference by claiming a camera wasn't working.

BF aside: He doesn't think it's a coincidence disturbing events happen and wants to get to the bottom of it.

It must be said that the alpacas were brought in as bait animals. This I believe amounts to animal cruelty as others have remarked.

1/ UFO News Article Utah Ranch Boasts UFOs Crop Circle Cow Mutilations
https://lights-in-sky.blogspot.com/2010/12/ufo-news-article-utah-ranch-boasts-ufos.html

SEASON ONE – EPISODE SEVEN – SURVEILLANCE

Surveillance: When a cow suddenly and mysteriously dies on the ranch, surveillance footage poses an otherworldly explanation.

***

HOMESTEAD ONE
AUGUST 16, 2019, 3.13 PM

There is a review of the current Homestead One bones in the basement saga. They put a microphone in the room. TT gives a half-baked idea that the room may be acting as an ultrasonic amplifier for drilling that will cause vibrations in eyeballs then causing people to see things and develop a flight or fight syndrome.

I would say this is an intentional sceptical strawman argument that seeks to reaffirm the main thrust of "anomalous phenomena"; in other words we are meant to be sceptical of TT's scepticism and be steered towards supernatural interpretation.

An helicopter appears and TW asks, *What's the purpose of flying over?*

Indeed, it is more grist for the Skinwalker Ranch mill. EB reports no transponder from the helicopter. Either he is misinformed about transponder regulations or the aircraft is breaking the law. And indeed, other than giving dramatic effect, what would be the purpose of a men in black flyover?

Royce L Robertson must be commended for doing excellent research on the subject of the helicopter. In the Skinwalker Ranch Facebook group I recommend, he describes how he contacted *Corporate Helicopters* who were surveying powerlines in the area.[1]

***

AUGUST 20, 2019, 3:41 PM

TT's trailer is filmed as he dramatically runs over to the cows. There is a dead cow, and as they vacate the area, TW's phone goes bizarre — as does KB's — seemingly correlating with the TriField meter reading 3 mW/m². TT says this is the same reading as one would experience inside a microwave oven.

JS reports a whole spectrum of microwave and AM frequencies on his spectrum analyser...

TT: *mankind doesn't know how to do that...* Really? This seem like more of the bovine stuff from TT.

TL and KL count the cattle. They wonder why they are clustering together. The cows had moved to the far West Field, away from the East Field where the dead cow was.

TT speculates about animals recognising microwaves more readily than humans...

Once again, the actuality of ETs or interdimensional entities inflicting microwave radiation on cattle, compared to possible human agency — if occurring at all — just seems so ridiculous an assertion.

I mean, haven't Skinwalkers and aliens got anything better to do?

AUGUST 20, 2019, 5:38 PM

Michael Gamble, MG, the vet turns up.

TW reflects on the effort of the vet compared to other cases of cattle mutilation. Is the diagnosis pneumonia ~ stress or a possible predator or microwave radiation?

***

COMMAND CENTER
8.02 PM

EB and BA report the day's events to BF...

BF announces he has an *expert* on these matters...

Here she comes folks...

AUGUST 21, 2019, 8:48 AM

BF aside. He reaches out to Linda Moulton Howe, LH.

LH, turns ups and the circus has arrived in town...

BF introduces LH to the team as the world's foremost expert. They take her to see the dead cow.

There are now picture asides of a *real* cattle mutilation. But in fairness to LH, she does suggest the stress may have come about by running. LH speculates on a new cycle of animal mutilations. She also pushes back animal mutilations back to the beginning of the twentieth century. This is always something to watch out for in *believing* ufologists: they always want to extrapolate back in time before 1947 to attribute anomalous behaviours. Yet there is no reason to believe the systematic animal mutilations from the 70s onwards occurred in previous eras.

LH has been an incredibly useful, *useful idiot* for the UFO circus. Her main strength is she seems to believe it all. She is a religious like fanatic that obviously basks in it all. In another age LH would have bought the wood from Noah's Ark, or purchased wood from the *true cross*. She gets to go all over and see different parts of the world; just like many of the cast from *Ancient Aliens*.

Since I first scrutinised LH, it seems she has moved further from being an unwitting disinformation agent to someone who at bare minimum must be suffering incredible cognitive dissonance while collecting all her *UFO dollars*.[2]

The thing is, from her own perspective she is promising *disclosure*. But this is the thing, it is the promotion of the *need for disclosure* that is the psyop. This millenialist like promise of disclosure taps into the religious like yearning of people within the UFO=ET religion; it taps into the desire of we human beings to look forward to something that offers deliverance from their present and often mundane, existences.

But you know, as much as I love science fiction — and I really do — I choose to suspend my disbelief of my own accord; I won't have the power to suspend my disbelief stolen from me.

AUGUST 21, 2019, 11:03 AM

The team and LH are assembled at the dead cow site.

LH recalls that the CIA and DIA reported similar microwave observations in their investigations of these phenomena.

TW wants to get LH's take on the alpacas.

LH asks whether orbs or beams of light have been caught on film.

COMMAND CENTER
AUGUST 21, 2019, 12:32 PM

EB shows some surveillance footage of a UFO in the vicinity of the dead cow.

1/ Royce L Robertson helicopter research
https://www.facebook.com/groups/1687428964648601/search?q=helicopter

2/ Getting off the Linda Moulton Howe CRAZYTRAIN
https://www.youtube.com/watch?v=EiUiF4KaISI&t=1s

SEASON ONE – EPISODE EIGHT – REVELATIONS

Revelations: The team learns their research is of great interest to the intelligence community - and share their findings with the attorney general of Utah. Season finale.

***

COMMAND CENTER
AUGUST 21, 2019, 1:12 PM

There is a review of the dead cow and UFO occurrence. The reaction of the cow to the object above her is discussed.

BF: *The cow reacted that moment that object appeared above the cow...*

I believe the cow died of natural causes or they killed it. On Skinwalker Ranch, unidentified helicopters and cattle dying — regular UTAH occurrences — provide ample opportunities for their own brand of spin and sensationalism. It is very likely that a UFO was superimposed on the film later.

Of course, aliens could have travelled light years to a kill a random cow in a field, but is it likely?

There is a review of the vet speaking of stress induced pneumonia.

The UFO seemingly displays an aurora. TT draws attention to in the famous *Tic Tac* video and references the AATIP group. A halo owing to a temperature differential is speculated upon. But of course, all the Skinwalker UFOs are ill-defined blobs of light and not well defined solid objects at all.

TT aside: He reminds us of BF's earlier briefing and BF seeing a UFO above the ranch...

TT, with reference to classified projects: *it could be a highly highly classified thing, but here's the thing: if there's a project that's that classified, that level of technology so far advanced from the rest of the technology we have on the planet...that's real hard to swallow.*

LH throws in some mystical stuff about portals.

***

ONE MONTH LATER
BF'S OFFICE, SALT LAKE CITY
SEPTEMBER 23, 2019, 9:36 AM

BF introduces Sean Reyes, SR, Attorney General, Utah...

The meeting is a chance to review previous experiences before SR, including TT's bone spurs, a cyst, and a picture of his finger.

TW recounts his history as well...

JS aside: He asserts TW's injury consistent with a radiation beam entering his head from behind...

TT mentions that *all of this is coupled but we don't know how...*JS says *yeah...*

We must remember JS's appearances are limited to the first series of *The Curse of Skinwalker Ranch.* JS looks uncomfortable. Has he begun to have had enough of it all?

TT speculates that the ETs might regard the rockets as *communication,* and wonders, *do we have permission to say "hi" back?*

EB and TT flesh out an idea that the basin is a reflective dish for radiation(energy) coming down from above.

BF: *What could be causing this energy?*

TT describes energy from above or below or both while in front of a graphic, accompanied by a balloon experiment flashback.

TT mentions being contacted by the *intelligence community.* This seems to be news to the rest of the team...

BF: *So we're being monitored.*

This is accompanied by a grimacing look from BA.

TT carries on: *There are real government institutions interested in this phenomena and are taking it seriously....*

The last observation is accompanied by a flashback of the *power line inspecting* helicopter...

Think about that: a TV programme is of interest to the intelligence community. What a load of hogwash. It's hogwash that this announcement could be any news to the rest of the team either. It's all scripted...

SR seems a little too smiley, as though he's in a school play. He is actually on a filmset and he plays his role very amateurishly. Given BFs position in the community, including the chamber of commerce etc., it's likely that SR and BF are well known to each other. SR may be playing his role in promoting tourism by giving an ear to the Skinwalker Ranch nonsense.

TT announces NASA will launch a rocket-satellite for free to observe the phenomena.

JS reiterates that *something going on, is coming from the ground...*

TT wants to take core samples...

BA chips in with his security remit speaking to whether TW should put himself in harm's way...

TT lays out his credentials as a *sceptic* who has been won over...

BF hopes this may validate the *something else...*

JS aside : He speaks of somehow signalling the entities

TT: *...Skinwalker Ranch may hold the secrets to the universe that we've yet to uncover...*

SEASON TWO – EPISODE ONE – BREAKING GROUND

The team recommences its search for answers on the 512-acre property; an excavation of a mysterious pit at Homestead Two leads to a frightening encounter.

***

The opening shots feature TV scientist TT reeling off his credentials for this news series. These include classified work with NASA. Now, anyone associated with NASA has to be regarded as dubious. After all, they have told one of the biggest lies of all time; yes, the fake moon landings.

TT asserts he has a better idea of what they're dealing with and this year they will find answers etc So straightaway, he is baiting the hope porn hook.

9.25 AM
Dr Christopher Lee, CL – a radiation

oncologist - is on board the chopper with BF. I mention in passing that the actor called *Christopher Lee* — more lately *Saruman The White* — often played Dracula back in the day. Whether the series makers are having a private joke at the expense of viewers by using this particular doctor, is an amusing thought. Oncology and a vampire's attraction to blood are obvious overlapping areas of interest...

BF aside: He reminds us of TW's injuries etc.

They assemble around the table .

BF mentions off-season events.

TT raises digging issue with the usual reprise of BA's reservations...

TT aside: He raises various *ideas* of what is underground...aliens etc.

TW mentions an hole near Homestead Two that drains water when put into it. There are suggestions of putting in dyed water and finding out where it drains; an idea probably copied from *The Curse of Oak Island*, and symptomatic of the show's scratching around for ideas.

***

HOMESTEAD TWO 11:21 AM

TT aside: He mentions fast drainage would imply it's going somewhere...

Casey Smith from Qal-Tek arrives.

The team disperses to various points to look for emergence of the green dye

12:44 PM

EB, BA, and Cico Silva, CS — the drone operator — go to the dry gulch area with a drone...

Thankfully, the skinwalker decides to allow

the drone to operate this time...

12.55 PM

The southwest fence line is visited by KB, KL, and TL.

HOMESTEAD TWO
1:13 PM

TT, CS, TW are still there...

TT aside: There is a flashback to drilling and telegraph pole shaking...

They look down this hole to see if green dye is still there, but they can't see anything.

TT aside: *We pumped about 45,000 gallons of dyed water down into this hole, and now it's just gone....*

No one is as good as TT is of creating a mystery out of a mole hill. Just fancy that, they pumped thousands of gallons of coloured water with no trace. Whoopee, big deal...

They check the cistern at Homestead Two but find no trace there either...

***

Meanwhile back with KB's team at the fence and EB's team at the creek, there's no green water detected at either location.

HOMESTEAD TWO
2:21 PM

TT aside: He reminds us of strange behaviour, including RB's team assertion of seeing portal and a creature emerging. There is a flashback of radiation sickness when the well/cistern cover was removed. CS, however, records low radiation this time.

***

COMMAND CENTER
3:26 PM

In a conference call with BF, the bogeyman of digging is raised again, and he *shows* initial reluctance to proceed as usual. But we all should know by now that BF's reluctance is like the circular band saw coming to cut Batman in half; a six year old may worry about the prospect of this of course...

BA gives the thumbs up though, and so the reluctant decision à la the soap opera plot is acceded to once more. The middle age female groupies can breathe a sigh of relief that ~~Batman will be rescued~~ and their favourite ~~boyband~~ experts will live to perform once again.

***

TWO DAYS LATER
10:43 AM

TT speaks while he is driving about BA being nervous about the coming dig...

BA turns up carrying a rifle. Why? OK, the rifle is clearly for dramatic effect. What's the inferred reason for though? Shooting skinwalkers or trespassers? The best defence against a skinwalker, as every member of the team should know by now, is to be armed with a camera...

BA aside: He goes over reasons for not digging etc.

TW removes branches from the hole with an excavator.

TW has three jobs on Skinwalker Ranch: to use machinery like a puppet from *International Rescue*, to be a handsome figure to be lusted over by middle aged female fans, and to *be injured by anomalous radiation*. TW is like a red shirted security guy from Star Trek who beams down to the surface. Their mutual prognosis is not good.

CS does a safety radiation sweep that proves negative.

KB's phone starts acting up as TW digs the dirt in the hole.

TT aside: He says even the NSA doesn't have the technology to hack phones. KB's phone is busy dialling random numbers... *currently even the NSA doesn't have the technology to hack that kind of encryption...*

How does TT know that? That is an assertion he can have no way of knowing. Are the NSA going to inform TT otherwise? He is a frigging TV scientist; he is a frigging construct.

TT: *something is crying out for help....*

KB*: Or is it giving us a warning...*

1:03 PM

TT: *Something here is crying out for help...* and he further asserts, *you can't hack the iPhone...*

From the point of view of the millions of female groupies of the show impressed by TT's handsome looks and paper qualifications, this is as solid as biblical scripture. It is wonderfully arrogant to presume technical knowledge beyond one's own expertise though.

TW say that phones playing up is not necessarily attributable to immediate or very recent actions; he recalls *delayed effects*. Well, *delayed effects* certainly increase the pool of anomalies attributed to dubious causes.

There is a reprise of cows, rockets and KB's phone.

KB mentions that the phone is being hacked while he's trying to change password...

TW carries on digging.

CS continues to measures radiation.

***

10:49 PM

While eating hamburgers outside TT's trailer, TT, EB, and KB, notice a yellow rectangular light... and then proceed to look for animal tracks?

Interesting that TT is *out of uniform* just wearing a tee shirt. The others are in uniform. It isn't clear to me that they are eating despite their being clutter on the picnic table.

TT aside: He wonders whether the digging caused all of this...

SEASON TWO – EPISODE TWO – CARVED IN STONE

As the mystery of a dead cow grows even stranger, a guest investigator alerts the team to a never-before-seen site that might hold the keys to unlocking the truth about Skinwalker Ranch.

***

The episode starts off with BF wishing he could get to the bottom of rumours of cave system below the ranch.

COMMAND CENTER
11:24 PM

TT relates to BF the activities of the *hamburger incident*.

KB mentions a rustling while TT mentions a shimmering orange yellow rectangular form 2 by 1 ft that was there and then wasn't.

This wasn't picked up by camera. TT says he saw a UFO after the camera was switched off.

EB shows frames of a horizontal streak that is interpreted to be something other than a meteorite.

THREE DAYS LATER
10:21 AM

Ryan Skinner, RS — *a researcher* — is brought to the ranch.

BF aside: He says it is important to bring in RS who has spent years researching the landscape and the property.

Bearing in mind the amount RS has churned out about Skinwalker Ranch — see Appendix B — it is a wonder he hasn't appeared more. I suspect they want to keep him close but not too close. RS is more of a fantasist and a grifter than *Prometheus Entertainment* can probably afford to entertain. Nevertheless, they feed him a few breadcrumbs.

RS aside: He recounts being chased by a ball of light...dropping his expensive camera etc...He fails to mention his encounter with the skinwalker that he describes in his ~~sci fi novel~~ *true account* of a previous experience at the ranch.

The team go to the NE corner of the mesa and there is mention of ancient pictographs on boulder that RS points out to the team. I find it difficult to believe he was the one who first found this independent of others. For one thing, his time on the ranch was always clandestine and fleeting. This sort of artwork would be well known about. There is also the question of whether this actually is ancestral artwork.

TT identifies the *Big Dipper* and *Draco* star constellations among the pictographs.

TT aside: He cranks up the mystery dial: *who carved this and what were they trying to convey?*

TT points out the pictographs may represent the mesa line with constellations included. He tries to correlate the experience of anomalous laser actions with dots on pictograph – he is stretching.

EB asks RS what stood out for him

RS asserts: *The triangle jumped out at me a little bit. The Shermans on the west side of the property would see a portal open up and these miniature triangles would come out of the portal and go over the property...*

Once again, the Shermans are being attributed to witnessing phenomena second hand. The *Shermans saw this or that,* is becoming something of a laughable phrase.

BF aside: *The Sherman family bought the property in the early 90s. It was their dream to <u>really</u> farm and ranch on the property, and <u>really</u> raise prized cattle... The Shermans quickly found unfortunately out that they were not alone...*

There is a picture of Terry Sherman in a 1996 newspaper. But why should BF need to emphasise *really farm* and *really raise prized cattle*? Is he warding off possible objections to the Shermans actually being in cahoots with the coming Bigelow project? Statement analysis would indicate the repeated use of *really* is deception.

BA aside: He reports on how the Shermans reported giant wolf type creatures and cattle mutilations. This is another second hand account attributed to the Shermans.

TW: *They unfortunately got chased off of this ground by the paranormal activity shortly after they took possession of the ranch...*

TT aside: He equates what RS related with what he saw the other night ...hmmm...

Back on the mesa in the present, TT asks whether the pictographs could be dated. EB chimes in with getting a glyph expert in to look at this.

COMMAND CENTER
1:12 PM

Dr Dean Taylor, DT, a vet from the Utah Dept of Agriculture is taken to see the dead cow, strangely enough, not disseminated by predators. He takes a sample from the carcass and later informs the team that obvious poisons have not been detected by the lab.

There is a flashback to 2019 also showing TW's mobile phone acting strange around the dead animal along with high levels of radiation concomitant with the whole thing. There are flashback with the UFO and LH.

TW aside: He relates how other animals have not touched the cow.

British investigative journalist, Richard D Hall is another animal mutilation researcher. He has speculated whether some sort of prion research is associated with the mutilation phenomena. Some may find this interesting.[1]

The team and DT are seemingly bemused by the non-attention of predators.

There is flashback of rockets being launched, and the bunching behaviour of cow along with UFOs. The cow died at the same time the UFO appeared, but the possibility of some photoshopping after the cow's death remains a possibility. Is any photoshopping the work of TL ? See Appendix B for speculation on this.

TT aside: *I'm wondering if all these event are related in some way, including what we saw the other night...*

What a detective... Though of course, TT is acting as a dot connector for the gullible groupies of the show.

DT seems to give a conflicting opinion on stress induced pneumonia diagnosed by the previous vet. The death, as reported, seems to sudden for him. He also mentioned that pneumonia wouldn't be the reason why predators wouldn't eat the cow.

KB observes there are no insects on the animal carcass either.

***

ONE DAY LATER

The team welcomes Dr Alan Garfinkel, AG, who is an archaeologist invited by EB

As they drive up to mesa, AG recounts his knowledge of paranormal activities.

He claps in front of the mesa; it is *echophonic*. This is something, we are told, native people would like: *the stones are talking...*

He identifies the serpent *Draco* as *guardian of a portal* – how convenient for the show's narrative.

AG tells them what they want to hear. Native people memorialised it all – apparently. Native Americans — and the Shermans — are an excellent group to attribute things to, since it is impossible to interview everyone and arrive at a genuine consensus view.

TT asserts *he is an astronomer* as he talks to AG about his observation about the pictographs.

***

COMMAND CENTER
4:18 PM

JM brings the Hicks family over to share evidence of UFOs etc., gathered by Junior Hicks, JH.

TT aside: He asserts that JH was the premier researcher of cattle mutilations and UFOs in the Uintah basin for over sixty years.

TW aside: He gives a biography of JH.

BF aside: He speaks of meeting JH, and describes JH witnessing phenomena predating both RB and the Shermans' residence...

We are shown photos of metal rods given to RB – but not given back to JH. Here is where TT seems to show disapproval of RB. It is described how RB scoured the field after learning of where the rods were discovered

JH's daughter Jani Lee Griffin, JG, describes a compass going funny, as well as seeing cattle mutilations herself. JH was a genuine researcher whom the TV shows is trying to leverage to gain credibility.

COMMAND CENTER
5:15 PM

TW relates how JH couldn't cut the rods. This of course is a reprise of the famous uncuttability of the materials mentioned by Jesse Marcel at Roswell. TW is playing into known folklore and can be assured of *nods of knowingness* from the faithful.

Could they be heavy metal rods though? Uranium perhaps?

TT aside: He describes how the Shermans sold Skinwalker Ranch to RB in 1996.

BA recalls that JH thought they may be energy cells dropped by a UFO. Interestingly, I don't discount atomic energy has a powering mechanism for antigravity propulsion myself. I give more details in *Fake Aliens And The Phony Nuke World Order*.

TT aside: He describes how RB team found *meta materials*; the way light passes through them is different from normal materials. TT speculates if they are related to UFOs, and whether RB has them hidden away somewhere, *will they find more of them on the ranch?*

And so, TT provides more fish bait to the watching audience.

COMMAND CENTER
10:06 AM

DT and TT link up over a video conference. Here DT says arsenic, cadmium, lead, or selenium are *not* present.

TT mentions to DT how high electric and magnetic fields were recorded around the dead animal. He asks DT if this could contribute to death.

Those interested might like to read Arthur Firstenberg's, *The Invisible Rainbow*. The book details the effects of electromagnetism on life.

DT says that he asked the lab if radiation would chase animals off, but he receives a negative response.

TT, TW, and BF asides: They try to connect everything up within their individual episode conclusions.

1/ Richard D Hall raises the question of prions within the cattle mutilation debate
https://www.richplanet.net/richp_search_menu.php ?searchtext=prion

SEASON TWO – EPISODE THREE – LASER FOCUSED

After a military investigator shares his disturbing report about the phenomena on Skinwalker Ranch, the team conducts a laser experiment, which leads to startling results.

***

COMMAND CENTER
9:53 AM

EB links a conference call to John Alexander, JA.

TT aside: He reports that JA is a retired colonel and a member of RB's team, the *National Institute for the Discovery of Science*, NIDS.

TT: *They investigated the ranch for over two decades, and this is the first time a member of the team has been willing to engage with us.*

JA relates how he was with RB when he bought the ranch.

BF aside: RB immediately locked the ranch down and established surveillance of the ranch. *And launched what was an unprecedented scientific investigation of the property...*

BF is never shy of a little hyperbole...

JA: *The old Homestead area is one that seems to specifically attract a lot of attention. One of the things that really stands out in my mind is that errr the observers are on the ridge line to the north and looking down on Homestead Two and they see a spot of light that expands and something came out about 6 ft tall...you know how dusty the roads are there, right? Well, something big came out, ran off, and yet you don't find any physical evidence of it...*

At this point or thereabouts in my study of the Skinwalker scam, it occurred to me to start attempting statement analysis on what many witnesses were actually saying. More detail on this in Appendix C where I pick apart certain claims. I will abstract various things said, and do my best to faithfully record the exact words.

TT relates events of something *stalking* them. But he can always be relied upon to continually connect the dots so as they *make sense* to the average viewer. In other words, he's spoon feeding the official narrative.

JA relates a *high strangeness, a high credibility* event. Why would he emphasise *credibility*?

It seems like he needs to persuade here. I refer the reader to statement analysis once again, and attempt a little soon...

JA also describes some creature akin to the eponymous sci fi *Predator* without him naming the film. The viewer is left to infer this. He continues now in response to TT:

Some of our people who are out late at night; this is in the winter, and they look up and there's something up in the tree; looks like it's above one of the cattle...

One of our guys has a rifle with him and shot; whatever it was fell out of [he hesitates here] *the tree* [we know the creature is in the tree; he is trying to be overly consistent IMO] *and disappeared totally* [Why the emphasis? *totally*, is redundant. Is this just narrative building?]

They went out the next day — I said it was winter and there was some snow on the ground — the one thing we found was this track that looked like a gigantic raptor... [undecipherable] *something out of "Jurassic Park" kind of raptor print, and we couldn't find any other tracks whatsoever* [once again, why the redundant *whatsoever*?]

Why didn't the shooters investigate straight away? Why wait for morning. Surely a flashlight could have detected a large print. *I said it was winter* seems to be an affirmation of his earlier *winter* reference and so seems to unnecessarily corroborate his own narrative; why not just mention it left a snow print and so just let the listener infer it was winter? So, why the extra effort to be consistent?

BA aside: He reports that given JA's history and past, he *sees no reason to not believe JA...*

Why should we need to be persuaded? In fact this was one of the most unconvincing witness testimonies given. Indeed, when I later read *Hunt For The Skinwalker*, I observed several book and TV discrepancies. JA's witness account is contrasted with the book's account in Appendix F.

TT asks JA what he thinks it is: *I'm not even sure how to begin addressing the complexity of that*...[because he is making it all up, and in this, he is truthful]...*it is my view that these things are all connected in some way. I would say they're... it is a portal...it's like multi-dimensional reality...and I think periodically the dimensions overlap and when they do, those are just as physical as you sitting there right now, but when it separates, it's gone...*

TT aside: Here he reprises his portal and Einstein reference with a flashback of the chalkboard wormhole graphics etc

As the call ends, TT mentions to EB if there is a wormhole it has to be *traversable with gravitational anomalies* and this is the cue for the introduction of lasers to the ranch; light bending etc The BS makes for a more *toys for the boys* episode of novelty equipment to be wheeled out.

***

SOUTHERN PROPERTY LINE
3:25 PM

The team construct an observation tower while waiting for the laser experts...

***

HOMESTEAD ONE
11:02 AM

TL, KL, TW tag the cattle that are arriving at the ranch. There is a flashback to rockets, a dead cow, and UFOs...

***

COMMAND CENTER
6:58 PM

Chris Novielli, CN, and Tim Anderson, TA, of *Nu-Salt Laser* arrive...

TT gets them to set up to probe areas of possible portal at Homestead Two in order to *poke the hornets' nest.*

TT aside: He reprises the idea of the Einstein light bending-portal to another dimension etc.

10:33 PM

The laser show is started. They face northwards towards the mesa from the newly constructed tower by the southern property line.

11:17 PM

They start lasering the mesa with multiple beams. They try and duplicate the earlier apparent beam split seen the year before by just using a single beam. No mention of course is made of the internal reflections that caused the laser anomaly last time.

***

ONE DAY LATER
HOMESTEAD ONE
11:18 AM

KL aside: She introduces us again to RS, who is bringing Kris Porritt, KP, a retired Unitah County Sheriff.

TL asks KP about how he came into contact with the ranch. KP says that he met Mr Myers. So we apparently have now a second hand witness to what the Myers *experienced* prior to the Sherman and RB ownership through their mutual fascination with horses. We are told they would ride together. For various reasons I believe KP is a liar.

BF aside: He reminds us that the Myers family obtained the ranch in the early 1900s.

KP says that Kenneth and Edith Myers spent the whole of their lives on the ranch and experienced unusual events on the property.

TL asks about locks on the property.

KP: *He had everything chained up. The fridge was locked, the cupboards were locked – even his car...*

When I asked him about all the locks he said, "Kris, I wouldn't appreciate you repeating what I'm about to tell you." And I said, "Your secret's my secret"...and he said, "I get visitors," he says "alien activity"...and he says "arr things come up missing, things come up dead.."

RS ask if Kenneth saw the aliens and what they looked like..

KP: *He could feel they was present, and he says I don't know exactly why they'd pick my ranch* [good question] *to pick on me...*

Indeed why would aliens travel light years to mess about with the Myers' cupboards and fridge. It's ridiculous.

TL asks about previous phenomena observed in the house.

KP: *Yeah, like screens on the window being taken out...And err, he'd tell me that at night time, he heard something stressful [while] he was sleeping*

TL relates *feeling being watched...*

TT aside: He discusses the alleged phenomena, which is accompanied by flashbacks from last year.

KP relates another happening:

What happened right here was one of the biggest tricks you ever seen in your life... Ken couldn't find three heifers. I got here just at sunrise with my horse. We rode all day long. I said "Ken, I don't know what to tell you about your heifers. We can't find fresh tracks, and he had a shed right here [he points], *and Ken couldn't get the door open...so they start pushing on it, pushing on it...I pushed as a hard as I could to the inside, and I looked in here*

...and I looked inside and said "Ken, you ain't gonna believe this. Your heifers are in the shed..."

They were stacked one top of each other like this...[demonstrates with fingers]...

Kenneth Myers tells KP they're dead, but KP get some water to be poured over their heads and they revive them. KP says snot was coming down their noses. They looked like they'd been drugged...

I discuss this incident in Appendix F – Discrepancies In Canon. I also reiterate that KP's account of the Myers' experiences is at serious odds with that of family member Garth Myers – given in the prologue.

TL takes KP away from Homestead One to meet the rest of the team.

***

12:36 PM

KP takes TL, KL and EB to where KP reported a previous cattle mutilation – not far from the recent cow's death.

He describes a classic a cattle mutilation along with an impression in the grass, *twenty three feet tip to tip, give or take a foot.* He adds *...I presume it was a spaceship...I said it, didn't I...* where he shows apparent self-consciousness about speaking of *spaceships.*

I must say, I'm not adverse to the theory that the deep state from time to time may have used antigravity technology as cover for their cattle mutilations. And there is no reason to equate these craft as being capable of space travel. In any case, I believe helicopters were often the preferred vehicle.

RS gets from KP that it was *cigar shaped...* and RS comments *like the Tic Tac...*Once again TT can be relied upon to be constructing a Skinwalker Ranch unified theory. The reference of course is to the famous 2004 declassified footage.

TT aside: He reminds us of the famous Tic Tac video and tries — he stretches — to link up the *Advanced Aerospace Threat identification Program,* AATIP, video with what has happened on Skinwalker Ranch.

KP tells how he's not the only person who's experienced stuff around here. He asks, *where did it come from?*

My first impression was that KP was a genuine witness. The heifer incident is so bizarre. I wanted to believe him. Once again though, just as we don't hear from the Shermans first hand, we don't hear from the Myers first hand.

Where are the photographs of locked fridges and cattle stacked upon each other? And for that matter, where are the really strange phenomena that are reported previously that is of a different kind from currently reported TV phenomena. There has been a dead cow; it wasn't mutilated in classical fashion though. Why aren't TL and KL now needing to lock their fridge?

EB has said previously that mutilations had been going on for over a hundred years but where are the citations? Newspaper articles etc...this is typical of disinformationists on the UFO topic who are often at pains to manufacture a continuity of ET presence prior to 1947 to validate extraterrestrial visitation rather than deep state technology accompanied by deep state counter intelligence machinations.

***

HOMESTEAD TWO
10:02 PM

EB aside: He speaks of orbs and portals *experienced before.*

At 11:02 PM, the laser rectangle starts up. The task is to see *bends* in light if they happen according to *Einstein's gravitational lensing* principle. Nothing anomalous, however, is seen.

Then they set up within the old house itself. BA and TT claim to experience a sudden temperature drop within the ruins. One of the two in the laser team half-heartedly corroborates. His team mate is silent. This silence is important. It corroborates my assertion that TT and BA lied about being cold in this building.

After shining lasers away from Homestead Two, they see a light in the Russian olives that TT and BA chase after but — unsurprisingly — disappears. TW and EB observe from the mesa. TW sees the light, but so does TT.

Is the *Prometheus Entertainment* production team responsible for the light I wonder.

BF aside: He gives out the usual stuff.

TT aside: *All I know for sure is that we need to keep exploring and experimenting* [and getting paid?] *until we find the answers...*

SEASON TWO – EPISODE FOUR – THERE'S NO PLACE LIKE HOMESTEAD 2

When a lidar scan reveals a dark mass at Homestead Two, the team invites a Rabbi to perform an ancient ritual believed to reveal inter-dimensional portals, which leads to chilling results.

*****

COMMAND CENTER
10:17 AM

As I was watching, the penny suddenly dropped that season two doesn't include dates. I believe the reason is this:

The — *Scooby Doo* — uniforms worn by the actors, and the possibility of filming many *ostensible days* in one day, would come under scrutiny if someone like BF spent all day in Salt Lake City but was recorded by *The Curse Of Skinwalker Ranch* as being in the Uintah Basin.

Pete Kelsey, PK, a lidar expert is introduced.

TT aside: He mentions a drop off of temperature from previously, seemingly corroborating BA's observation. Indeed, one of the laser operators was recruited to lie about experiencing a temperature drop as well.

TT aside: He discusses PK's assignment to get a 3D image around Homestead Two. He also reprises the various claims made about the place.

PK explains lidar as a way of mapping 3D images. He tells EB to use the lidar scanner to *just paint it* in order to collect the data.

EB goes in and around the old house at Homestead Two with the scanner and *paints it...*

COMMAND CENTER
1:35 PM

TT aside: He goes over the Junior Hicks material accompanied by a flashback.

Roland McCook, RM, is introduced as a Uintah Basin native. Skinwalker Ranch was about two to three miles away from his house when he was growing up – or so he tells us.

JM calls him *a close friend and confidante.* That RM turns out to be the most obvious liar and exhibitionist to date, must surely beg questions about JM himself. JM is another man with a cowboy persona who has real estate interests. I have to say though, he does have fantastic waistcoats. He has been the fashion star of the show...

RM: *What I saw has haunted me for years* – regarding time up on the mesas...

In the Homestead Two area RM says he, *feels a little nervous to be honest.*

Why would he need to be *dishonest* though?

RM is with JM and TL, who asks him how it all started:

The weather was moving in and we was looking for a place here, to shelter and get out of the weather. We came in here, and I didn't really want to go into...all the way into the building...hmmm...but the person I was with, he said "come on in, let's get in...into the building," and so we went further on in...and... when we got in there... well...while we was waiting, I was looking out of the door and I heard ehh.. like ...scurrying...[he describes the sound] *something moving... and I turned and further in that back corner* [pointing] *some stuff fell over... it got knocked over. I told him that's something bigger than a raccoon... I took off, grabbed my gun, and out the door I went after it.*

RM aside [interposed with above and below – why?]: *We thought it was racoon to begin with; racoons or squirrels or mice running around, and things started getting knocked over, and that's we thought......there's something else going on here... and then you get...that creep... kinda creepy feeling like there's something more...*

[RM continues what he's saying to JM and TL in the present filming take]

We were looking...looking for tracks. We noticed there were human footprints [the sound editor puts in large *boom*] *...no shoes on...it was like human footprints...*

JM: *In the snow...*

RM: *In the snow, yeah, and I... followed the tracks, and then all of a sudden, they turned from human footprints into a big dog... Tracks... like... a wolf* [he gesticulates with upturned palm begging to be believed perhaps?

The sound editor interjects another *boom]*
and it came out, red eyes, probably nearly eight ft
tall, and then it just pointed, pointed at
me...whatever it is, it doesn't belong here . We
shoo...started shooting...(semi-automatic [unclear]
) [He makes sound, *pop pop pop pop*] *and all I*
hear is the biggest roar [he makes the sound
quietly]...*loudest roar I ever heard, and after that...*
it just... it was just gone [gesticulates with arm
movement]...*We took off...*

JM responds by saying that the word is that
this [Homestead Two] is the gateway for these
shapeshifter and skinwalkers...

RM responds...[looks around]: *yeah...*

JM aside: He reprises the story of the Navaho
and the Utes, and how the Navaho cursed the Utes.

BF aside: *The Sherman family who lived on*
the property in the 1990s; they encountered these
giant wolf like creatures that the native Americans
would refer to as skinwalkers. It started attacking
their cattle, and were literally impervious to err...to
gunshots...

Back at Homestead Two, TL asks RM, *what*
happened after that?

Hesitates...*Got home...*[He omits the
pronoun *I*] we *would...*I *would* [further pronoun
confusion indicating deceit] *hear things at*
night...things at the window. I'd lay down, put the
pillow over my head, they'd come around; you
could hear their hand or claws, just like going
across the building...growling the whole time...and
it still...you know...that...it...the vibration and
everything right through to your soul...I just
like...what if we do....Hold on

[he semi collapses onto TL's shoulder, who
grabs hold of him , and he seems distressed. JM and

KL ask him if he wants to move away. On one level the BS is comical.]

No, no I think I'm OK [He walks away supported by TL.]

TL aside: He believes RM nearly passed out, and mentions the place of nearly passing out is by the cistern.

RM aside: He continues from earlier: *What I saw, I think it was a skinwalker, and the feeling that I got, the fear I had of it, came back; that's hard to explain*

And back in the present RM says: *If you wouldn't mind guys, I'd like to be here by myself, and yeah, have a moment...a little bit of closure.*

[JM, TL, and KL move off as RM walks around]

RM aside: *I knew I needed to come back here for me to get this closure* [this is narrative for when we see him walking around the Homestead Two site] ...and he explains the sage burning ritual...

Interesting that he is not alone during sage burning at Homestead Two; the cameraman is around for one thing. The soundman too picks up his *stayaway prayer*. At this point we may not only reflect that cameras and sound also work, but nothing detrimental ever seems to happen to the cameramen.

JM aside: As RM finishes off sage burning JM says *he hopes he will bring closure* etc

***

3:13 PM

EB aside: He decides they should, *load up and see if they can find anything...*

TT aside: *We don't know whether this gentleman had a medical issue or what, but given my experience of Homestead Two...we brought Geiger counters, dosimeter, and TriField meters out there in case unusual levels of radiation could be detected...*

The interesting reference to a *medical issue* suggests that RM's antics may have been a bridge too far even by the usual Skinwalker Ranch production team standards.

So, the team including TT, TL, KL and EB convene at Homestead Two with measuring equipment.

TT registers high magnetic field and comments, *we're getting neutron counts that I don't think we should be getting...*

That's a new one: *neutrons.* They must have been searching their atomic particle lexicon for hitherto unused nomenclature. TT sounds like Spock on the bridge of the Enterprise, continually perplexed by novel alien forms and energies...

***

ONE DAY LATER
COMMAND CENTER
9:32 AM

PK sits around with TT, EB, TW, and BA

The 3D image presented allows for viewing from different perspectives...

TT aside: *Where we should be seeing the inside of the main house, it's just a black hole*

Skillfully playing into the wormhole-gravity rhetoric. Of course, just because the lidar is not giving what might be expected is no reason to jump to paranormal explanations is it? And might we expect future attempts at Homestead Two with the lidar? If not, why not? Surely this is the scientific method, but each episode seems to need the new novelty of different technological devices or new *spiritual experts*.

Indeed, up to the end of series two, we never get to see another attempt at lidar. It must surely have been a low labour and cost effort to repeat this experiment. Of course, the viewership isn't bothered; it suspends it's disbelief and demands new novelty, technologies, and visiting experts.

TT observes that when EB walked in the building, it didn't take any data.

EB looks *perplexed*. EB's look of being perplexed is a similar look that BA expresses when TT chunters on about Einstein and black holes etc.

EB: *Guys. I walked for minutes inside of these rooms. There should be tons of data here we're not seeing.*

At a timestamp of [21:13], PK gives EB a sideways glance that looks like, *who are you trying to kid?*

EB is an under reported and very qualified, experienced, *real scientist* compared to professional *TV scientist*, TT. Could he have switched the meter off intentionally in order to further the *black hole theorising – aka BS-ing*?

Might we expect PK or someone else to repeat EB's failed scanning in the house at Homestead Two? What about the scientific method vis-à-vis repeating experiments? Did PK refuse to go into house with scanner because in order to give *Prometheus Entertainment* the result they wanted, PK would have to compromise his professional image in view of future employers? By sending in EB, PK has plausible deniability – perhaps.

TT aside: *Since the slam scanner seems to appear to have gotten good data everywhere at Homestead Two, except inside the old house. I don't know how to scientifically explain that...*

Do it again then "Mr I-Am-A-Scientist" Taylor...His middle names is "speaking-as"...

TT aside: He reprises JA portal at location etc. He also mentions that strange behaviour goes back over a century. This repeating of the, *over a century of strange behaviour,* is a frequent mantra, observed more by its continued assertion than by much evidential backing.

***

THREE DAYS LATER
COMMAND CENTER
5:38 PM

Rabbi Ariel Tzadok, AT, the founder of the *Koshertorah School*, and an *Ancient Aliens* regular, arrives at the ranch.

TT aside: He suggests that since conventional methods seems to have hitherto been exhausted, it's time for a new approach.

Around the table TT mentions that AT had mentioned that Jewish faith looks at some of these phenomena differently from the Christian faith. In an aside and around the table, AT gives the patter about entities described by the Bible

The Old Testament is common to Judaism and Christianity. So how can Judaism give an answer above and beyond that of Christianity? It can't, but it does of course get another *Ancient Aliens* journey man onto the *Prometheus Entertainment* payroll of course.

The thing is, people have been bending the Bible to whatever message they want. It's such a vast document with many contributing authors; it's possible to get the Bible to say practically anything you want it to say if you are selective...

AT: *You could actually have portals opening and closing on this property with a living non-human intelligent entity; coming and then disappearing; coming and going...*

TT aside: He mentions that AT has told him that rabbis have knowledge of tonal technologies to open up portals etc

What a load of BS.

AT: *We're going to create a sacred place, and do the traditional prayers for opening of the gates. We will specifically invite whatever is here, if it's willing, to communicate...to show some sign...because these entities are out there... I already sense it...*

At timestamp [26:09], just after AT finishes *that* sentence... TT points out a UFO (light) in sky

TT looks up for no reason as though expecting it !!!!! He has no reason to look up if he is looking and listening to AT. It looks like he knows to look up or is slightly told to. This is either divine synchronicity or utterly contrived BS. Contrived in the sense that the UFO or drone with reflector etc has been timed to appear at exactly the right time perhaps or even that the end of the sentence provides someone to get busy with Photoshop and colour in a new orb into the edited footage. This scene is a major smoking gun to the falsehood of *The Curse Of Skinwalker Ranch.*

They *load up* after EB's suggestion to go to Homestead Two and, *talk to it....*

AT finds a *good rock* and announces they will create a sacred space for an entity to appears if it wants to. He makes some gestures with a walking stick with a gold metallic end to it, and asks them to place some rocks around him. In fact he does something of a Gandalf impersonation.

***

8:45 PM

TT aside: He tells us that he is informed that this particular tonal ceremony is only effective if performed after dark. Riiigghhttt...

AT gives traditional evening prayers.

TT notices some, *anomaly of heat signature,* in the doorway of the house at Homestead Two – what a surprise – not.

10:49 PM

AT: *That's usually an indication of a presence...*[with respect to the alleged *cold signature*] *... these entities are always being described as being very cold...*

Is he making this up as he goes along – could he give biblical chapter and verse on this I wonder? In any case, just because a screen indicates coolness and an actor report coolness, is there any reason to believe the screen or them? As mentioned before TL's skills in computing are not especially advertised. Is this because he is the *Photoshop And Equipment Anomaly Man?*

BA reports on never feeling a difference like that before as they walk around Homestead Two with flashlights.

TW makes a good suggestion of doing 4 or 5 nights to get a baseline...will this suggestion be taken up – as suggested by a *non-scientist*. I'm surprised that this made the cut. TW speaks some sense here. The same of course could be said of the failure to attempt another lidar mapping.

***

THE NEXT MORNING
COMMAND CENTER
10:38 AM

TT aside: *...The 20 degree drop in the old homestead was <u>undeniable</u>...*

Why assert *undeniable* instead of just mentioning it? Why the need to convince? OK, I deny it happened.

EB shows that the thermal imaging shows coolness just after AT's ceremony. I don't believe it.

Previously when I was wondering whether the ranch may have been showcasing various microwave weaponry, I speculated that three explanations could be offered. The first I automatically discounted.

~~1/ The area become cool because of an *entity.*~~

~~2/ The area become cool because of technology deployed as part of the Skinwalker Ranch psyop~~

3/ The witnesses are just lying about coolness, and the thermal imaging equipment has just been calibrated in order to give the narrative required.

Suffice to say, the third option is what I am convinced is what happened. When TW mentions being hit by *a wall of cold* when entering one of the buildings at Homestead Two I began to realise that they were all pretty much telling lies. Week by week my original idea that they may have been showcasing weaponry receded as I realised they have all been lying most of the time.

...And you have to wonder — to use the stock phrase of *Ancient Aliens* — if all the phenomena are as portrayed, why a filming company are allowed to

present all of this as entertainment when the deep state would surely wish to keep the public ignorant of such matters? Indeed, the introductory narration describes the federal government — by sponsoring NIDS — of being defeated in their exploration of Skinwalker Ranch phenomena.

A private filming initiative succeeds, but the federal government with a bottomless pit of finance fails. Come on, how likely is that, really?

EB shows the apparent swift movement of a cold particle across the bottom of thermal imaging screen.

In the looking ahead at the end, TW mentions being *electronically attacked* and wanting to leave the ranch.

Now given TW's observation of being cold and his previous (alleged – with medical pictures), I had previously supposed one of the following was true:

~~1/He has absolutely no idea what's going on.~~

2/He is an actor who has faked everything.

~~3/He is an actor who has faked to some extent but also been a victim of energy weapons, and he may be showing his exasperation with his handlers...so TW might be paid a lot of money, and the TPTB might have some leverage on him too , but this is just speculation on my part...~~

Given JM's acquaintance with RM, TT's implausible looking up in the synchronicity (contrived) moment, I came to revise my initial estimation of the various people at Skinwalker. While watching *The Curse Of Skinwalker Ranch* I initially believed that some were dupes and a few were *in on the psyop*.

I now find it hard to believe that some could be actors and some dupes; after all they work and live together. The more of them that seem suspicious, the more likely it seems to me that it can only be a team conspiracy. QED, they are all actors.

Electronic attacks against TW or radioactive attacks against TT would have pissed them off if real. And if the attacks were real then TW and TT are truly idiots. But they are not idiots, they are conmen. I now doubt all the minor players in this show as well. I recall TL said of RM, *he's the real deal;* why wouldn't he be the *real deal* though? Why the need to persuade unless if he wasn't the *real deal*?

And if TL and KL are actors, their claim to hear strange noises at Homestead One must also come into question. Indeed, *Prometheus Entertainment* may have decided that it would be more practical to get them to make stories up than employ others to put the heebie-jeebies on their ranch caretakers. From a legal point of view, it might be preferable too.

Indeed, why are we not reminded of the caretakers' unease at being in a location with apparent paranormal activity? There has been no stakeout of Homestead One in two seasons. Why aren't there sensors and monitors in the caretaker's house?

I was willing to let go the observation of some scripting as the team interact, but in real life people repeat themselves and mention redundant details; notwithstanding the need to edit out this stuff. The scripting thus seems to go further than what might be regarded as acceptable in a real documentary, but seems more like actors carrying forward a science fiction script.

A big deal seems to made of PhDs, experts, and so on. AT mentioned he was a rabbi not a scientist. TT mentioned he was a physicist. So there's an identity proving exercise employed against viewers. While scientists are lauded, scientific method in terms of repeating past experiments is not. There seems to be a worship of scientism and disregard for science. We must trust the experts in their accredited fields.

Experts can be bought off.

SEASON TWO – EPISODE FIVE – THE RANCH STRIKES BACK

A thermal experiment at Homestead Two reveals more evidence of a strange presence, the team is suddenly affected in dangerous and disturbing ways.

***

The flashbacks as usual are not accompanied by any new attempt to get a lidar image of the old house at Homestead Two. This is a gigantic red flag. They could have tried to duplicate the anomaly or rule it out by another attempt. In the event, there is an unnecessary question mark about a survey that could have been swiftly repeated.

COMMAND CENTER
10:44 AM

There is a review of the alleged cold object moving across frame of the thermal image of the doorway of the old house.

TT tries to equate this object with the alleged monster emerging from *a portal* seen by the NID's guys. But then again, this fallacious *dot connecting* is something that TT routinely does.

TT aside: He reprises John Alexander's testimony.

The team, at TT's suggestion decide to replay the rabbi's ceremony with more equipment present. OK fair enough. Why not do the lidar again as well then? As it is, the *rabbi experiment* is only performed once more.

What ever happened to repeatability and the scientific method from "Mr I-Am-A-Scientist"?

1:23 PM

TW picks up Steven Wall, SW, a supposed nephew of the Shermans.

As they drive, TW asks SW how long it's been since he was on the ranch

Almost...almost thirty years I believe...

And TW asks him about his feelings about coming back on:

Nervous; just anticipating; just seeing it; seeing if it's still the same...

TW aside: He tells us that SW is the nephew of Gwen and Terry Sherman and lived for four years on the ranch when a child. This among much else is at odds with the account given in Knapp and Kelleher's book, *Hunt For The Skinwalker* – see Appendix F – Discrepancies In Canon.

BF aside: He reprises the alleged strange happenings, and that these events motivated them to sell the property

SW, prompted by a question from TW about how he feels, says:

It does. Right now I have a lot of emotions going through me right now...it's bitter sweet I guess coming back though...

SW aside: *I lived here as a small child. There was some crazy bizarre things that happened that I can remember as a kid that...I just remember feeling a little scared, a little nervous...*

TW and SW get out of the car and SW is introduced to EB, TT, and BA.

EB asks SW if he could say anything about the places around here.

EB aside: He mentions he has never had the opportunity to speak to the Shermans.

TT asks about vapourised dogs:

SW: *They weren't vapourised, they were compressed into the ground...*

TT asks further:

SW: *Like something heavy smashed them* [He accompanies with his foot coming down, and downfaced palms pressing down]

SW in answer to BA: *Yep. From what I remember, a blue orb came bouncing down* [he points in the direction] *off them rocks right there...*

TT: *They believe a blue orb killed the dogs...is that what you're saying?*

EB asks SW if this was something he was told or witnessed...

SW: *I saw it with my own eyes* [The underlined was spoken very quietly. In any case, with whose eyes would we otherwise expect him to see it with?]

SW aside: *When I was a kid, me and my uncle saw something coming down off from the mesas. As we were we standing by the house, there looked like bouncing ball and orb, I guess you would call it... it was like a blue colour* [Was it blue of whatever shade that could be attempted to be described or not? This sounds like storytelling to me]. *I remember hearing the dog whimper, and then I remember finding the dogs SMASHED. I don't really know what happened, but I just know man couldn't do that.*

It's curious isn't it that cattle mutilations and the killing of dogs ascribed to aliens begs the question of why ETs wouldn't have any scruples about killing humans.

EB and others ask about circles in the vicinity the of dogs...

SW says, *It looked like something hot sat there in the weeds...*

TT aside: He speaks of the difficulty of believing but recalls the orange-yellow glowing of four weeks previous.

***

They now head for Homestead Two.

In the car SW mentions how it all *got crazy around here* ... They are just by the mesa...

It all focused around this, right here.. [He taps on the car window to emphasise]

12:36 PM

Outside of the car:

The first story that I can really really hardcore remember: down there there's a gulch [A vee shaped valley] *..OK...right over there you could see something open up there in the sky...something came out of it; a peach coloured object, OK. Me and my uncle saw it come through the field.*

But, it came working its way up through [He points and sweeps around] *them Russian Olive trees and it came up and just scouted these trees just like this. It came up, went over the canal and it drove down the path of that road right there...*

EB suggests the object might have displayed *scouting behaviour.*

SW continues, *Like they were... they were... searching through the trees. And it went straight up* [He turns and points up at 45 degrees] *and that hole closed* [He turns to face EB as hands clasp tight]

Consider:_really really hardcore remember_ Why the emphasis? And here, *You could see something* – why not use *I* or *we* rather than the third person *you*? See Appendix C – Statement Analysis, on personal pronoun usage.

I don't believe his narrative.

TT goes over this as an aside with respect to *portals...*

It has to be said that the UFO portals ascribed to Skinwalker Ranch are uncommon as far as I'm aware, but it is common to ascribe high speed, high acceleration, and high maneuverability to the many observed UFOs themselves.

TT aside: He mentions the sincerity of SW. OK, TT is trying to persuade us. In the last episode TT mentioned possible mental issues with RM. Since TT is about as insincere as you can get, his vouchsafing of *sincerity* is comical.

***

THE NEXT DAY
4:34 PM

Guy Blocker, GB, is introduced to the team.

TT aside: He explains how they will replay the rabbi's chanting, taking new measurements with more tech, and also use *old school* thermometers in the homestead.

EB aside as they film the location setup:

Look, this is a really speculative exercise. When we start talking about portals and such, but in this particular location on Skinwalker Ranch, anything is apparently possible. And if we do in fact cause some of this phenomenology to manifest, we absolutely want to document it...

***

8:45 PM

They set up.

TW and KB go up the roads from Homestead Two to be in a better place to see the object that was seen last time.

They then start the playing of the recorded rabbi chanting.

TT aside: He asserts that the temperature of the image analyser increases as the recording progresses and says, *It was crazy; just like a switch got flipped...*

GB seems to confirm that the rise from 38 degrees [Fahrenheit] to 47 degrees [Fahrenheit] is not normal.

TT aside: He *reluctantly* seems to accept the rabbi-portal explanation in his reflections...

GB aside: *Wasn't really sure what to expect. I've got to say I was quite surprised by what we did encounter. It's been the first time that I've been in a place using thermal and watch the temperature change so drastically.*

I don't believe him. He's someone else on the payroll.

KB and TW see a light from a window at Homestead Two. There's a lot of excitement as they run to the corner of the house where they find a thermometer knocked to the ground. The most likely explanation is someone has gone in with a flashlight and then put the thermometer on the floor. The thought of why there aren't any surveillance cameras present also comes to mind.

Inside the house, they see something moving outside and give chase. In one shot TT is running forward towards the cameraman at timestamp [23:12].

How did the cameraman get there first? Perhaps he's the one that caused the commotion?

Although in the previous films aspect after TT shouts, *I'm on my way,* the flashlight is in the other hand. So, it might have been filmed after for dramatic effect. One might argue that there's nothing wrong with a little creative editing and asking the actors to film a shot again. OK, if this is an argument, but don't try and then say this is a scientific documentary.

In any case, as TT catches up with TW, the flashlight is now back in his right hand as they observe and ponder going into the bushes. They claim to see something moving.

TW: *What I saw was 6 ft diameter* [He gestures with arms spread wide]; *really intense and then it kinda got dimmer as it like went out a little bit, like it faded. And while I* [was] *sitting there staring at it trying to figure out what it was, it started to move like this* [TW moves sideways]. *And it just kind of moved across, and then it was like it just disappeared into the trees, and that's when we...*

KB finishes: *...yeah, it was right through there....*

TW aside: *Whatever it was that we saw tonight; these were seen only with the... the thermographic cameras, and we couldn't see them with the naked eye. And that tells me that we're not dealing with something necessarily that's physical. Eh, we could be dealing with something that's another dimension or another realm. So I know at for a fact it was not an animal and it definitely was not a human; beyond that ...eh...you know, your guess is as good as mine.*

Well my guess is that it was just people running around at night with flashlights if it was anything at all...

***

THE NEXT MORNING
COMMAND CENTER
9:10 AM

TT aside: EB calls BA and TT to show them surveillance data from the mesa while they were conducting experiment on Homestead Two. The mesa seems to light up; BA observes it has a history of doing that on that particular section...

As they are discussing this, TW interrupts that something popped up on the Wi-Fi and its unsafe, *and then it kicked me off of my computer too...*

Almost certainly a scripted interruption.

TT mentions to EB that they would see any hacking on the spectrum analyser.

Suffice to say, TT recollects from the previous year, 2019, the signalling, and they flashback the wormhole blackboard episode.

TT aside: *I'm an astrophysicist who has been researching and studying this possibility of these kinds of phenomenon for more than 25 years, but I never thought it would lead me to a ranch in Utah, contemplating the existence of wormholes...*

TT: *We're actively being electronically attacked; right there...*[He points at the screen]

10:27 AM

TT, points at the screen at a regular signal and says, *that is a transmitter somewhere doing that...*

TT goes over to his trailer.

TT aside: He describes how EB has put directional antennas onto his trailer, and how they can be pointed to detect where any signal is coming from. The current source is found to be coming from the mesa's southwest, and the signal is overpowering the network.

Meanwhile, in the Command Center, TW is not feeling well

TW: *I'm leaving the ranch. I'm getting a bad headache...*He is asked, *are you serious?* and he replies, *I'm dead serious...*

BA and TT aside: They reprise TW injuries from the past.

TT tells EB in the Command Center that the signal appears to be moving...

EB aside: *The fact that the source seems to be moving is pretty mysterious; it's kind of suspicious. It's suggestive of something artificial. We don't know whether we're talking about something on the land or in fact, in the sky above us...*

TT and EB communicate back and forth as the source apparently moves while EB tries to see what's around the ranch with the cameras...

TT aside: *...there's a transmitter designed here in a way I've never seen* ... [Mr Spock, again]

TT in his trailer asserts, *there is so much structure to it that it's clearly something hmmm ...*

Here TT appears to suffer from some [microwave radiation] attack...

I was just suddenly short of breathe...like I hit pause or something...it was so weird...all of a sudden my thought was not there...I couldn't finish what I was saying...that was freaky weird...

Originally when giving the benefit of the doubt to the Skinwalker players, of course, I believed they may have been targeted by 5G weaponry.

BA goes from CC to check on TT. TT then goes into the nearby metal silo to block out radiation...

TT: *Holy...*

BA: *Did it go away?*

TT: *... like a damn switch...*

BA reports that he himself feels as right as rain.

When TT comes out of silo he feels fine....

TT aside: *I had this weird static electricity feeling all over my body. My... my... skin was tingling, my hair was* [sic] *felt like it was standing up...more than usual, but when I came out the last time, I no longer felt that feeling. That's not a coincidence...*

They bring up the spectrum analyser and can no longer see the structured signal, observing that *it just looks like noise...*

They call TW and get him to come back to the ranch.

TT aside: He asks why it affected TW and himself but not the other guys.

The simplest answer is laughably simple: It is because TT and TW are just making stuff up.

SEASON TWO – EPISODE SIX – SKIN DEEP

An investigator presents the team with evidence of a mysterious cavern system running beneath the ranch.

***

COMMAND CENTER
10:11 AM

James Keenan, JK — an *investigator-writer* — is introduced to the team...

TT aside: He mentions that EB invited JK. JK performed vector magnetometer surveys of surrounding areas and says, *what he found, pointed him here...*

JK describes how his compass just kept on spinning, *faster than a second hand.*

EB aside: He mentions other witnesses to this phenomena.

I'm unaware of this phenomenon being demonstrated to the viewers of the show.

JK makes a presentation of magnetometer readings.

TT aside: He comments that background is usually something of the order of 80 micro Teslas, and not the -40 micro Teslas that JK reports. He speculates as to the presence of a void, *or even an underground structure.*

JK describes how the three anomalies describe a straight line through Skinwalker Ranch. He says, *I believe there is something underground.*

TW aside: He reprises the rumours of previous accounts...

The line cuts through the *Triangle.* The Triangle is of course three converging dirt tracks that the production team want to attribute Bermudaesque characteristics to. The location owes its delineation to some questionable triangulation carried out by TT and others in the last series.

TT aside: He reprises the balloon along with the portal account, and he contrasts the above-below ground debate on the origins of the *phenomenon.*

No one can add up two and two and get five quite like TT can.

JK suggests some underground water passage.

TT aside: He opines magnetic effects may be the result of heavily mineralised water.

Not being an expert on hydrology-geology this myself, I would nevertheless say that this would be a well-documented phenomenon within that field. No doubt there are specialists in this field. Why not invite a specialist along to the party?

JK suggests a grid search that they then embark upon. He conducts a magnetometer survey, calling out readings to EB. He reports an *anomalous oscillation* of readings that according to TT, *shouldn't happen...*

TT aside: *Something strange is definitely going on below this Triangle Area...*

12:11 PM

JK reports the magnetometer reading is dropping. EB reads back, *31 to 49*. As lay people we have no idea what this can possibly mean. The best most of us can do is suck up the hyperbole generated by the team.

***

COMMAND CENTER
1:44 PM

The caretakers run cattle footage past EB. The images seems to show a UFO blur there and then not there on alternate frames; they observe that cows left a particular area and didn't come back...

Again I wonder whether TL has used some of his *IT-Photoshop* knowledge. This I can't prove for sure, but I do mention it. As far as the show itself is concerned, the rest of the experts don't avail themselves of TL's IT expertise.

If I had been part of the team's production team I may have given an advertised IT role to TL to anticipate scrutinisers like myself. In negating his skill set, the producers thus beg the question as to what TL is otherwise doing on the ranch.

EB shows cow tracking data with the hot-cold technique. It seems the cows avoid the area in which the cow had previously dropped down dead.

TT aside: He speculates about whether the dead cow was related to something in the air or underground.

***

BA and EB welcome Zak Zyla, ZZ, a Ground Penetrating Radar, GPR, expert back to the ranch.

ZZ says he can realistically measure 6 to 10 ft underground – perhaps more.

And so, GPR is performed in the Triangle Area.

12:02 PM

ZZ: *That's going crazy...We're putting out an electromagnetic signal under the ground and the ground's really making the whole thing ring...*

This asserts ZZ, is because the soil in the earth is highly conductive.

TT aside: He agrees and adds the alternative of mineral laden underground waterway as well.

ZZ also suggest that there has been a section of digging and then back filling.

The consensus seems to be that digging is required with the usual BA aside of circumspection...

***

ONE DAY LATER
10:44 AM

The excavator heads toward the Triangle Area and starts digging.

TT aside: A spectrum analyser, gamma radiation detector, lightning strike meter, and a metal detector are to be used to the monitor area as they disturb the ground.

TT uses a metal detector which works and then doesn't work as earth is removed by TW in the excavator.

Clearly the metal detector has been another *working/not-working* prop to parade before the always functional cameras.

TT aside: *The deeper we dug there, the stronger the signal was getting on the metal detector, but we found no metal object at all in the spoils at that point...so it made me think, we must be getting closer and closer to a really large metal object or structure...*

TT reports that the metal detector was malfunctioning...

BA aside: He reprises the exotic underground base theory...

***

THE NEXT DAY
COMMAND CENTER
9:53 AM

TT aside: He tells us that before they can dig any deeper, a greater survey is necessary. So *Juniper Unmanned*, specialists in lidar and magnetometry, are invited: *To give a deeper a more comprehensive survey of the ranch where we keep seeing anomalies.*

TT draws our attention to all the coloured water near Homestead Two that went missing and the possibility of an underground waterway near the Triangle Area; hopefully the magnetometer may provide some answers.

***

HOMESTEAD TWO

Drones are flown with an attached magnetometer device that may find stuff 100 ft underground.

TT aside: He says that they spent the best part of the day conducting a magnetic survey of the Eastern Field, Homestead Two, and the Triangle Area. He says, *they pretty much covered the whole ranch..*

***

COMMAND CENTER
TWO DAYS LATER

Nathan Campbell, NC, and Jeff Cozart, JC, of *Juniper Unmanned* give a conference call to the Skinwalker team.

There seems to be a strong magnetic reading near Homestead Two. The Triangle Area shows signs of possible tunnelling...

They call BF.

***

10:38 AM

BF arrives by helicopter from Salt Lake City.

TT aside: He mentions the anomalous areas near Homestead Two, the Eastern Field, and Triangle Area.

BF asks what they have discovered that should make them want to dig in those areas.

EB mentions the strange behaviour of metal detectors.

BF aside: He reprises his reluctance — for dramatic relief no doubt — of digging and disturbing the earth. Of course, this is obviously one of the repeated soap opera memes.

In the meeting, BF shares that Ryan Skinner has gained confidence of the Sherman family, specifically Gwen Sherman. Gwen told them of an exact location on the ranch *where not to dig...*

Google map show the coordinates to be on a rock. The rock seems to be about ¼ of the way from Homestead Two towards the Triangle Area...

There are now lots of asides about digging on the ranch.

The great anti-climax of *digging where they shouldn't* will be revealed next episode. Suffice to say, the production team had obviously been scratching their head for some sort of plot. But in a way, the negative findings along with repeated — nay monotonous — experiments should be the real fayre of a genuine research project. Alas, it is apparent the Skinwalker faithful on Facebook often describe their distaste at the slow moving nature of *The Curse Of Oak Island* – a favourite of mine.

Alas, the Skinwalker TV watching faithful want to be entertained and carry on surrendering their suspension of disbelief to accompany their sofa snack scoffing TV brainwashing.

SEASON TWO – EPISODE SEVEN – CAN YOU DIG IT?

While conducting a drilling operation at the Triangle Area, the team not only detects dangerous energy spikes, but also discovers something that may have come from outer space.

***

8:11 AM

A drilling rig team moves into the Triangle Area from *Pete Martin Drilling*. They are Fernando Rubio, FR and Troy Black, TB.

TT aside: He mentions previous findings: magnetic anomalies and a possible water course below. There is the supposition of an artificial tunnel system. The show's actors always tantalise the viewers with the expectation of fantastical underground discoveries, be they flying saucers or lost cities etc.

Cynics will observe that if fantastic discoveries are made, the show's presentation of them will of course be pre-empted by announcements on national news before the season's episodes are aired. The willingness of show loyalists to continue in their self-inflicted suspension of disbelief must surely have its origins in the otherwise mundaness of their own lives.

EB briefs the drilling team.

EB aside: He suggests something might be provoked. They never tire of saying this...

***

RANCH ROAD
8:22 AM

TW moves in with the excavator to *the place they shouldn't dig...*

They turn over the boulder, dig, and find nothing. Readers might appreciate the anticlimactic, *Story Of The Auld Empty Barn* as told by the character Private Frazer in the British sitcom, *Dad's Army*.[1]

KB speculates that an image underneath the rock may be a thunderbird pictograph. This allows the producers to edit in a little bit about native American folklore, but the suggestion is pure speculation and is not held on to. Any *symbol there* is just imagined and random lines in my opinion. There is a condition called *pareidolia* that describes the need to see faces in clouds and similar random distributed forms.

In fact, Facebook fans of the show continually exhibit pareidolia in interpreting Google Earth imagery as buried flying saucers etc. This is comical but also sad. Many people will perform real mental gymnastics to try and twist reality to a more interesting version they want to believe in.

9:38 AM

KL is inside a dug hole and takes a look around...

***

TRIANGLE AREA

10:23

It is starting to get wet at a shallow depth...

***

EAST FIELD

10:42 AM

This is where the cow died.

TT aside: He recalls how *Juniper Unmanned* detected circular anomalies in the ground.

The Skinwalker team are very keen on the use of *anomaly* and *anomalous*; it fits the mystery selling point of the show. The thing is, surely everything in the natural world can be construed as anomalous given that natural features will always depart from imagined mental constructs of how things are or should be...

TT aside: He recalls the dead cow and the alleged UFO...

***

TRIANGLE AREA

11:16 AM

At 25 ft they have drilled into flowing water.

Flashback aside: The disappearance of coloured water is again mentioned.

They call off drilling and move to another point on the Triangle...

***

EAST FIELD
11:49 AM

TT goes over dug dirt with the metal detector but doesn't find anything...

TT holds a measuring tape into trench and claims it is being pulled into the side by magnetism. OK, why not get a magnetometer? It's not very scientific from the man with six degrees is it? This is complete BS.

TT aside: *The ground and the pit we dug and where the cows have been avoiding is strangely magnetic. What makes it really freaky is that there's no large metallic objects or structure of any kind buried here that we can see.*

TT goes on to relate how EB's original conjecture about magnetism emanating from underground can be tied in with various phenomena; such as TW's head episode etc. They decide to dig where Kris Porritt reported a mutilation.

Flashback aside: We see footage from season two, episode three featuring KP.

TT aside: He accentuates *the weird* magnetism in the ground. Once again rather than attach superlatives, he should attempt to get precise measurements.

As KL, KB, and TW stand around, TT attempts a hypothetical grouping of all observed phenomena under the umbrella of electric current in the soil...

***

LATER THAT DAY
THE TRIANGLE AREA

They are drilling hole number two.

EB aside: He explains the working of a spectrum analyser as being sensitive to electromagnetic waves. It allows us to see what frequencies and at what amplitudes the surrounding radiation is. An unaccounted for frequency is seen. The drilling rig is temporarily switched off, and it is eliminated as the culprit because the anomalous frequency still registers on the instrumentation.

***

EAST FIELD
1:23 PM

KB and TT want to see if there any energy readings owing to all the digging. TT says the gamma readings are about three times higher now than normal background in the vicinity of the dead cow site. I don't recall ever seeing footage of gamma radiation instrumentation or hearing any rapid Geiger counter clicking.

TT mentions a continuous magnetic field going on that should be zero.

We only have TT's word for it, which is not worth much.

***

TRIANGLE AREA
1:23 PM

EB points out a *strange frequency* on the spectrum analyser again. He describes the active peak as *moving around*, giving a *waterfall style plot*. He doesn't know what's driving it.

EB aside: *We seem to be receiving some kind of energy* [sounds like Star Trek]. *We think there may be an energy source nearby that could be interpreted as artificial. I wonder if this is somehow connected to the drill...*

***

EAST FIELD

TT and KB claim their compasses show magnetic north shifted by five degrees toward drill rig. They go to observation point at the southern point. The filming and use of compasses seems to be a little suspect at best to me. I go over in detail certain compass antics of TT and BA in episode nine. The interested reader might like to watch the episode here on a frame by frame basis to see if TT and KB are telling the truth.

OBSERVATION TOWER
1:56 PM

TT now allegedly observes a fifteen degree anomaly in his compass reading.

***

KB and TT go and join EB and the rest of the team at the Triangle Area.

EB and TT view the frequency modulation.

TT aside: He reprises the recent occasion when he and TW didn't feel well from extraneous radiation. And he wonders whether the digging and drilling is causing the various radiation to kick off again.

EB and TT compare notes.

EB aside: He equates these new anomalies with the fact they have never drilled so much before.

RB had twenty years with millions of dollars of government grants. What did they get up to if they were genuinely seeking to explain strange phenomena? Surely they would have done *some* digging?

Once again, if their research is *classified* then why would the government allow new owners to take

139

the property and make a *scientific documentary* about Skinwalker Ranch?

You have to conclude any classification owes itself to the nature of RB's work rather than the specific location of Skinwalker Ranch.

BA corroborates TT's and KB's compass readings...

THE TRIANGLE AREA
4:47 PM

The second hole is not muddy at 25 ft. They dig down to 70 ft then to 100ft, and discover something that is possibly gilsonite, aka asphaltite.[2]

They play up the possible meteorite origins of gilsonite that also fits in with the extraterrestrial connection meme. Others doubt the assertion that gilsonite is created by meteorites while others accept it.[3,4]

***

COMMAND CENTER
10:26AM

EB informs them of the chemical analysis: strontium, barium, manganese, and iron etc

According to TT if you were to crush up an aircraft, these are exactly the materials you would expect. But, as someone in the reddit link says, bearing in mind minerals come from the ground, this really is an asinine statement to make; nevertheless, TT's observation derives a — contrived for the cameras — *look of wow* from EB.

S2 – E7 – Can You Dig It?

1/ The Auld Empty Barn
https://www.youtube.com/watch?v=Qr_v_SqJNjA

2/ Gilsonite
https://en.wikipedia.org/wiki/Asphaltite

3/ Gilsonite and meteorites
https://www.reddit.com/r/skinwalkerranch/comments/
o67a3o/gilsonite_is_not_evidence_of_a_meteor_or_as
teroid/

4/ Gilsonite and meteorites continued.
https://www.distractify.com/p/what-is-gilsonite-
skinwalker-ranch

SEASON TWO – EPISODE EIGHT– SHOCKING REVELATIONS

When the team uses high-powered Tesla coils to shoot electricity into the oddly conductive soil of Skinwalker Ranch, it stimulates an otherworldly encounter.

***

The recovery of gilsonite a week ago is reviewed.

HOMESTEAD TWO
2:33 PM

They build a circuit that will run from the well through a battery and multimeter to a grounded conducting rod that will show the conductivity of the soil.

BA inquires of TT and EB as to whether the conductivity may in some way explain the strange feelings people have had. TT says that we still don't know where the hidden power-battery source is.

EB aside: *I've wondered for a long time whether there might be some kind of underground energy* [Star Trek speak] *source. Some people have expressed a belief that aliens are somehow involved. And we may be on to why a conjectured alien civilisation or some ancient earth civilisation may have used the area as a power storage...*

The meter shows approximately 280 mA and this draws exclamations of incredulity.

Using ohms law and assuming the battery is 12 volts: resistance = voltage/current = 12/.28 = 42 ohms.

The website *Circuit Globe* gives this graph for a spread of ground resistivities.[1]

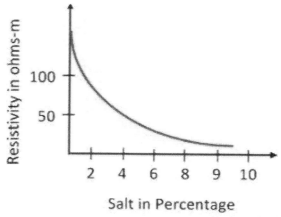

Salt in Percentage

Circuit Globe

As can be seen, 42 ohm is a fairly mid-range resistance value that is being hyped up by TT.

TT: *I tell you what. What we are seeing here is a phenomenon not a lot of people have a good grasp on.* [And TT will play on that ignorance.] *This whole area is acting like a power supply. And it's storing up power, and then we're suddenly letting it go when we disconnect from the car battery. And as it's draining out quickly, it looks like a lightning bolt.*

As part of the drama they light up a flashlight. All this seems quite disingenuous: they use a battery to pass a current and then try an infer there is an extraneous power source. Surely they should keep the same circuit and remove the battery?

This is all pure BS. TT in an aside describes how much warmer he is to the alien hypothesis than when he first came; strange comment since he has appeared regularly on *Ancient Aliens*.

All this sets the show up for what TT calls *a much more aggressive experiment*. So putting a giant Tesla coil in the ground is suggested. Despite EB's understated science credentials, he always seems to be following TT's lead with exclamations of *wow* and studied expressions of amazement when the former speaks.

We may recall EB is a reserved character based on his biography given in Appendix B, whose credentials are scarcely mentioned at all while *Dr Know-it-all*, TT has a whole Wikipedia page. If EB and TT were a comedy duo, EB would be Henry McGee and TT would be Benny Hill. EB seems like TT's straight man.

And while one might expect editing to cut out the incidental, the way the team interact without the interplay of plot-extraneous speech and movement, more and more suggests a scripting beyond what I originally anticipated. The problem is not scripting in the small sense, but scripting in the larger sense.

And once again we have the pretext for the introduction of more show novelty looming —
without carrying on with previous experiments

including the question of whether Homestead Two "allows" a 3D imaging survey — and we can look forward to the visually impressive and sci-fi style Frankenstein lab prop, the *Tesla coil...*

And of course, BA as the show's doom monger has to insist on conferencing with BF. It amuses me how the shows' groupies resent BA's studied inertia when it's all actually part of the soap opera.

Of course, we may expect that the trio of BF, BA, and TT will reprise the roles of inquiring conservatism, the reluctant servant of permitting doubtful practice, and the flamboyant Alabaman black belt in karate respectively.

***

ONE DAY LATER
12:56 PM

BA wears his shades as he overviews the landing of BF's helicopter.

TT suggest the layering of conductive and not so conductive layers is akin to a battery; possibly an explanation of the *underground power plant* idea. This is the rationale that is put to BF.

BF asks if this is normal while EB backs up TT's claim of strangeness.

TT aside: He describes Tesla's work including his desire to transmit electricity across the world.

TT speculates that the ranch might be something like a *UFO recharging service station.* Of course, this is what the faithful love to hear. He is full of it.

BF aside: He describes how he has seen strange stuff: An image from Jan 19 2018 1:41 AM is shown of a moving light-UFO; a video, December 23,

2018 5:52 PM of a laser like beam being shot up into the air from the mesa; and January 19, 2018 1:41 AM, images of the mesa being illuminated.

BF also mentions the Shermans witnessed UFOs. He has seen UFOs with his own eyes along with multiple witnesses. This I don't necessarily doubt; it's their interpretation that is moot.

After TT tells BF he wants to use the biggest Tesla coil he can get, BF wonders whether he can handle the potential power unleashed [as predicted]. BF defers to BA who then defers to TT – the narrative of course being the ongoing acceptance of the *reckless* TT by the *conservative* BA.

BF asks how soon the equipment can be brought over. And from TT's answer — see below paragraph — it seems as though it has already arrived or is as imminent as to make the usual three way debate an obvious scripting of the usual dig no-dig discussion. The faithful will easily identify the *physical triangle* but fail to identify the *soap triangle*.

TT : *Well, I've talked to a colleague of mine; he's ready to bring some equipment out, like now; I mean, any day now* [slightly muted on *now*] *so...er...we're right now, looking at the Triangle Area to do the experiment...*

TT aside: He mentions sending a lot of electricity into the ground etc.

***

Now, I myself only really noticed the casts' uniform changes later in the series when TT wore a dark greyish shirt in the after show asides. I've also seen him with the same background doing interview material for William Shatner's show. I mention this and much more about TT in Appendix B. It also seems odd to me that the background is deliberately blurred.

***

THREE DAYS LATER
9:38 AM

This episode is where I first noticed the *Scooby Doo* type uniforms that the cast always wear. I'm sure other may have noticed well before I did. I put the below paragraph in parenthesis as it represents an earlier revelation to me I had while watching this episode. Of course, the frigging around with ostensible dates and days — including the compression of multiple days into one — is facilitated by their *Scooby Doo* attire.

(TW, TT, and EB are wearing the same coloured shirts as three days previous [striated light grey/blue, mauve/navy blue, and cream] Either they are all fairly unhygienic people, they have different shirts, or the shirts were washed and decided to wear the same shirts as three days previous. In all likelihood, they carried on filming while the Tesla coil crew were outside and TT,BF, and BA were engaged in their usual scripted soap opera...)

TT talks to Cameron Prince, CP, the Tesla coil engineer about how they should proceed.

CP aside: He explains how the coil is an air core transformer that takes up AC voltage and boosts it up to create the lightning.

They go to Triangle Area.

TT describes that since strangeness occurs at night, it would be best to conduct their *experiments* when the sun went down. Of course it would, the dark gives more cover for the film crew to put on their monkey suits and go trick or treating with their flashlights.

At this point I would like to make the observation that their shadows seem to be lying very roughly west-south-west to east-north-east, with the mesa to the north. This is consistent with the next scene when its dark four hours later. I mention this because I start looking at shadow direction from now on to see if they corroborate the supposed filming times.

***

FOUR HOURS LATER

CP mentions he's never ran the coil at the level of power they are about to. As Scotty would say, *The engines cannae take it captain!*

They start off with the smallest of the Tesla coils, and put light bulbs in the ground. As the dial is turned the bulbs light up.

10:33pm

The Tesla coils give off a yellow purple discharge.

Apparently there is nothing unexpected according to EB's instrumentations, and so according to TT, *It was time to up the ante...*

TT aside: He says that maybe they can stimulate some kind of communication or get a response.

After the big coil is switched off, they claim they can detect, unaccounted for, anomalous readings.

KB aside: [the security guy remember] reports that as he was watching the spectrum analyser and watching these strange signals [Star Trek speak] coming back. Not wishing to be a science snob, but unless he's been especially trained, how can he make the *strangeness* call; notwithstanding, CP says he's never used that power before.

The so called noise floor [TT explained as phone and tech etc.] remains high.

The thought occurred to me that elsewhere away from Skinwalker Ranch a controlled experiment with the same coil and settings could have been done to establish a baseline for this equipment, but of course they don't and they won't.

With regard to spectrum analysers, CP say there is no way that coil can produce that frequency. So either: He is mistaken, there is some extraneous radiation, or ET and skinwalkers are responding...

TT: *The ground is somehow acting like a transformer, turning low frequency lower power into higher frequency higher power*..

CP: *How is that possible?* [it seems like bad acting as he says this]

TT: *daa.. tha.. at...it at...it*... *means there's a transformer under the ground or something*

From my understanding of statement analysis, the redundancy of the underlined would suggest TT is just waffling.

CP aside: *We typically see a very strong resonant frequency of the coil and a couple of harmonics right near that, but one thing that was really odd is, we saw much higher frequency, high up in the Mega Hertz range, far beyond what the coil normally produces...You know, I can't explain this signal, but it did seem to be affected, or provoked, or started by the coil...*

Once again, there needs to be a controlled experiment off the ranch.

EB: *But here's another thing, I can't keep that quantum number random generator number program up...it continues to shut down on its own...*

TT: *wow*

There's some back and forth between EB and TT about the spectrum analyser. EB says that the apparent anomalous readings don't correlate with the Tesla coil being switched on...

TT: *I have tested that device to fly in space...*

EB: *OK...*

TT: *Cause I'm about to fly four of em on the space station in December...and..*

EB: *So that should lay that concern to rest right away...*

TT: *It shouldn't be that...*

EB aside: *Some of our instruments have clearly been interfered with. And I'm asking myself whether this is an indication of stimulus and response; are we dealing with something that is technological. Is there an "other" on the other side of the interaction? We all want to know the answer to this...*

By this stage in series two it had become clear that the only interference taking place was from the team of *experts*.

***

COMMAND CENTER
THREE DAYS LATER

TT aside: He explains he is aways from the ranch for a few days, but continued to monitor the footage from the camera on his trailer. He wants EB to got to footage of 2.30pm-ish when there was a thunder and lightning storm in case there was anything else happening. But the footage doesn't seem to show it...

Was this thunder and lightning claim just a pretext to get to the possible UFO that would have been a suspicious call if TT had just claimed to have seen a UFO?

EB plays back TT's footage but there is no lightning. They do however see some object in the sky. From that they then trace the same object falling/flying from one of EB's cameras.

BA underlines my observation but gives it a different spin by referring to it as *a huge coincidence.*

EB tries to correlate this with the previous Tesla coil experiment based on their ongoing assertion that the ranch doesn't necessarily respond straightaway to their shenanigans. Bearing in mind TT is always stressing the scientific method, the removal of causality beyond the normal range of time intervals expectations seems like *non-science – nonsense* to me.

***

COMMAND CENTER
1:30 PM

There is a conference with BF about footage. BF agrees with EB about a causal connection with the Tesla coil experiment.

1/Circuit globe resistivity graph for salty soil
https://circuitglobe.com/earth-resistance.html

SEASON TWO – EPISODE NINE – LOOK, UP IN THE SKY

As the team launches high-tech rockets into the mile-high zone above the Triangle, unidentified aerial phenomena suddenly appear.

***

I watch *The Curse Of Skinwalker Ranch* via the Blaze TV channel here in England. Having deleted some of my notes by accident, I was forced to purchase this episode via Amazon Prime. The first thing I noticed was instead of the usual English accented narrator, there was an American one. I'm not too sure why Blaze TV goes to the extra trouble, as I can't say I find an American accent offensive; indeed, the show has a fair few of them...

RANCH ROAD
8:11 AM

TT aside: He gives the rationale for what they

are about to do above the Triangle Area. He mentions the high conductivity of soil and a number of UAPs. The faithful groupies have also abandoned the term *UFO* for *UAP* to be in step with their idols.

I observe the *Triangle Area* is obviously a designation that will resonate with those mindful of the *Bermuda Triangle*, but other than the dubious triangulation measurements that pointed to this convergence of three dirt tracks, the Triangle Area just seems look a hook on which to attach phenomena.

TT gives the Skinwalker team a prep talk in the presence of the team that have brought along some big rockets. We see some flashbacks of previous rocketry and the supposed consequences.

The rockets will cover a range from 2000 to 12,000 ft.

BA aside: He describes the excitement of the rockets.

BA gives a lecture on the possibility of odd things happening to the rocket team and tells them they should report any strangeness occurring in their lives. TW chips in on this vein as well, as does TT.

HOMESTEAD ONE
10:30 AM

The caretakers greet Ward Hicks, WH, son of Junior Hicks, JH. JH was a local science teacher and a well-known compiler of UFO — *sorry I mean UAP* — data and witness statements. The American southwest has clearly been a testbed for the trying out antigravity craft. WH takes them through a number of cases.

TL tries to relate the work of JH to his own

sightings from the ranch. More stretching of course.

COMMAND CENTER
1:42 PM

They prepare the rockets with the various detector payloads while TT gives a prep talk about looking up at the sky. BA chips in with the fact that they all have cameras on their phones.

EB aside: He describes the three team approach to the rocket experiments. It will comprise of the three man rocket launch control, the team on the mesa, and the retrieval team.

TT initiates with the old 5-4-3-2-1 countdown. The production team have tried to create the ambience of an old style Apollo lift off.

Apollo had a significant amount of fakery, but that's a topic for another day; suffice to say that anyone who believed Armstrong walked on the moon is an idiot or a disinformationalist. Where one stands on the moon landings, 9/11, and the 2020 scamdemic is a good indicator of one's truthseeking credentials...

No UFOs are seen. KB's phone starts going awry again. His code is *broke in three tries*. Bearing in mind much else that goes on, it's likely that KB has been issued with a dodgy phone that can misbehave on cue.

A second rocket is launched that goes a mile high. It is equipped with gamma ray detector and camera. No high gamma radiation is detected. The next rocket will have transmitter on board and dosimeter. CS calls out a UAP that TT states is at the same spot as last year.

TT, in Captain Kirk mode, tells them to go with *rapid fire* on the remaining rockets. Meanwhile

Dave Barber, DB, of rocket team reports the hair on his arms standing up. The film team focus briefly on him before he reports. Are they anticipating the witness he is about to give?

DB: *Do you guys feel that?*

Others: *no...*

DB: *I don't understand how nobody else can't feel that. I don't get it...*

BA: *Look at his arm*

DB: *It is not cold out here.*

BA : *Something's up...*

DB aside: *So, we hear Travis on the radio uh, say "hey, I think we saw something up there", and huh, my eyes just kind of lit up. I'm like "yeah, well, I'm feeling like my hair is getting almost pulled out." My hair on my arms would just stand up...It was kind of weird; it was a fast wave but it was a very intense wave.*

Interestingly, BA on the radio reports that DB is experiencing *magnetic anomalies – how does he know they were "magnetic"?*

DB aside: *There's definitely something going on but we had a job to do; we had to get rockets in the air and get the instruments up, so focus up, get to work.*

DB and colleague are filmed making ready for new launch...

DB: *That's so crazy. I can't believe nobody else can feel that.*

Other rocket guy: *I got something else going on too now bud.*

DB: *Okay, well good. Making me feel like I'm [not?] a nutjob.*

So why does the *phenomenon* only affect one, two, or a maximum of three people at a time?

Why don't camera men ever experience anything? I believe it's because the producers can only direct and edit a couple of bad actors at a time.

At TT's instigation they get ready to launch the big rocket, and he goes to his trailer to monitor the spectrum analyser.

EB explains to DB what tech is being put in the big rocket payload.

EB aside: He describes how any deviation from the norm of the transmitted signal may be picked up by TT and his spectrum analyser.

The rocket is launched and TT reports from the trailer.

TT: *Oh my God, during launch, the electromagnetic spectrum is going crazy, guys. I've never seen anything like it...*

He continues to radio from his trailer to the rocket launch site.

TT: *You wouldn't believe what I'm seeing on the spectrum. I can't wait till you see this data. It's absolutely unbelievable.*

Just then EB's spectrum analyser dies.

TT reports that there's no explanation for that and there are flashbacks of the Tesla coils not functioning etc. Of course, we are lead to infer that the *phenomenon* is the culprit.

6:18 PM

A slight flap occurs as the rocket opening chute isn't seen at first. The production team really milk what is only a small delay.

DB: *Here we go. All of a sudden we're...Yep, nope. Whoa, whoa. That's a big one – heavy.*

EB: *I can see that..*

DB: *My legs, too...*

BA: *There's <u>absolutely</u> something going on right now...*

Why the need to persuade with *<u>absolutely</u>*?

BA aside: He reasserts a *magnetic anomaly*.

Presumably, security training involves magnetic observational skill these days. The team decide to swap DB around with a colleague. The exchange of personal gives an opportunity to set the mesa up for night time rocket launches.

10:33 PM

During the rocket launch there is a brief burst of lightening.

We see TT and two others, and hear their exclamations.

At timestamp [34:21] we hear *What is that? Lightening. Yeah lightening...*

EB aside: He mentions he wants to examine this from the perspective of the surveillance cameras.

***

ONE DAY LATER
COMMAND CENTER
2:02 PM

BF flies in, timestamp [35:40]

The shadow of the helicopter is consistent with an early morning shadow being cast in an ESE to WNW direction. I say this because a *time shadow discrepancy* will be noted in the next episode.

As it is, they have a round table recap with BF about the previous days' events.

EB suggests the appearance of an orb may be a response to their rocketry.

Once again I suggest there has been some photoshopping to make this claim good. Originally I wondered whether drones may have been employed or lights on a balloon. Bearing in mind the whole production team and team of experts are liars, the simplest and most economical method is simply to edit the film and insert bright yellow blobs. And it must be said that none of the ~~UFOs~~ UAPs has displayed any structure.

There are no saucers, triangles, or cigars. The days of the wheel hub cap being photographed only occur in the fayre provided by the hoaxer Billy Maier who's testimony is still garnering the old UFO dollars. Yes, believe it or not, there are people more stupid than those who believe *The Curse Of Skinwalker Ranch is real* ...

SEASON TWO – EPISODE TEN – IT FOLLOWS

It Follows: As members of the team investigate the Triangle Area using Brandon's helicopter, they are shadowed by an invisible entity.

***

COMMAND CENTER
12:33 PM

There is a conference call with BF and CF about the coming helicopter experiment over the general area of the Triangle Area.

TT aside: He reminds us of past *phenomena*.

They reassure CF there will no *emission* of radiation, just the *measurement* of gamma and microwave radiation.

CF mentions that as soon as there are any problems he will land the helicopter. Of course, he is saying this because he knows what the ruse will be. In the episode where we first see CF he says a little prayer – what a BS artist.

Bearing in mind the whole Mormon sect is built on lies we shouldn't be surprised perhaps. I feel the same way about most organised religion but Mormonism was clearly built on the specific hoaxing of Joseph Smith.

***

ONE DAY LATER
COMMAND CENTER
10:44 AM

As BF and CF arrive by helicopter, BA reprises his concern about experiments.

BA greets the Fugals with handgun in holster to fight off any brazen skinwalker attack. They then convene outside.

EB aside: He describes how the helicopter will helix to different heights above sea level: 5, 7. 8.5, and 10 thousand ft. The location is already 5000 ft above sea level, so 7000 ft above sea level for example, corresponds to 2000 ft above the ground they're on.

As TT describes the fitting of the spectrum analyser and Geiger counter to the underneath of the helicopter, we see film of TW and TT fitting the tech for an instant. This is no doubt to create the illusion of TW and TT being *hands on guys*. The footage of this is momentary and we can't witness them discussing the work in hand or what size wrench to use and so on.

TT mentions the 10,000 ft level has a potential source. It is therefore 10,000 − 5000 = 5000 ft above the ground — approximately a mile up — where *strangeness* was detected with the rockets. He mentions dangerous energy spikes and UAPs.

As they climb, one altimeter shows them being only 40 ft above the ground for some reason that causes subsequent consternation. This, it is suggested, is a big deal.

It is CF who takes over the role usually played by BA. He expresses uneasiness etc., and they decide to land.

ABOVE THE TRIANGLE
12:11 PM

CF reports the haywire altimeter to ground control.

At a timestamp [12:49] we do see a simultaneous view of the ground below with one altimeter showing 45 ft while the other shows 4500 ft (9000ft above sea level.)

EB aside: *I don't have any indication that there's a source of radio frequency energy at 5000 ft above the ranch. I don't have any support for the idea of a gamma ray source. What I do have are unsettling indications that we may not have been alone up there. I don't know what to do with that, I don't think any of us know what to do with that.*

We have to assume that one of three causes is in play:

~~1/ There is something stealth like   an invisible flying skinwalker or an alien craft underneath them.~~

~~2/Something   is   interfering   with instrumentation. 5G telecommunication systems being one culprit.~~[1]

3/They themselves have interfered with the meter.

***

Since 5G can possibly interfere and EB and TT are so called *scientists*, they should certainly be aware of this more prosaic possibility if they are aware of the more exotic blackhole-wormhole-porthole BS theory.

The possibility of human agency is never mentioned. There is no thought about outside operatives. And they seize upon there being a radar return based on something underneath without even considering an instrumentation failure. CF says it's like someone is following us. This is pure hyperbole.

EB mentions that one of the first things he wants to do is reach how to BF.

During the course of the flight TT mentions a spiking of gamma. My thinking when I first saw this episode was that gamma claim was invented by him, but the microwave~5G may have been genuine.

After watching two seasons I'm convinced all ostensible anomalies are attributable to equipment doctoring, the use of imaging software, and simply telling lies.

***

TT's TRAILER
12:53 PM

In a conference call with BF, CF interprets the reading on the radar altimeter as meaning there was something underneath the helicopter.

***

ONE DAY LATER
COMMAND CENTER
2:07 PM

BF arrives by helicopter and a convenes a meeting to discuss the *next steps...*

EB aside: He reports that on reviewing footage from previous rocket launches, *we are seeing more than meets the eye.*

He shows the meeting an apparent orb on the screen. And says it appears and disappears. He shows 13~14 on the same day. Time stamp [21:46]

I asked myself the question whether this was genuine or video editing. I strongly believe this was edited in after. As such it betrays the whole modus operandi of UAP sightings and led me to consider the reality of the supposed more solitary blobs of light in the sky.

Curse Of Skinwalker Ranch

It Follows

Series 2, Episode 10

BF ejaculates *what* when EB shows these.

Bearing in mind these occurred on the same day at different times with most people out and about at launch control, on the mesa, or rocket recovery, how come only the one they all see together is the one initially of note?

Certainly, if the orbs flashes were momentary not all would necessarily be seen, but *surely more* would have been seen and noted. How come EB is only mentioning it now? If real then why the delay in processing and mentioning it; camera surveillance and viewing the footage is EB's job.

Further, it looks like a blue filtering effect from dark to light has been applied from top to bottom; I'm not saying this wrong, I'm just making an observation. I did the same when changing a photo for a book cover when I needed to provide contrast for white lettering.[2] The point I wish to make is that if *Photoshop* or some other imaging software is used on still photographs — I use the free version called *Gimp* — then why wouldn't they use it for more illicit reasons?

How come EB wanted to *reach out to* BF straightaway earlier but has only just done so with multiple orbs? These orbs were supposedly filmed a week ago. And by the same token, is BFs ejaculation of, *what*, merely bad acting?

Just as EB is enlarging upon the discussion of UFOs, the cows seem to be running quickly to the other side of the field. Very convenient for continuity; reminiscent of when the rabbi said he felt some sort of contact was imminent and TT looked up and saw an orb from the same vantage point of the convened team.

The strange phenomena seem very beneficent in allowing one segment of the episode to come to a natural end before directing the programme in a new direction. This has happened several times when the team has convened on the outside porch.

Why don't fresh happenings occur when they are eating or drinking coffee or making small talk?

But do I wonder in this instance if someone had dumped a stack of freshly cut grass. I have seen this myself. Cows can move very fast when food is on offer, inclusive of being allowed access to new pasture if gates are opened. The caretakers say they've never seen the cow behave like they have just witnessed. More hyperbole in my opinion.

2:36 PM

TT aside: *The magnetic field on the ranch was suddenly double what it should be. I..I just have no way scientifically to explain what in nature could cause that...*

We see no video of the magnetic readout, no matter how fleeting. We just have to take his word for it. TT's word is worth nothing. It doesn't matter how many letters you have in front or behind your name.

BF to KL and TL: *Have you seen them react that way*

They answer almost simultaneously...

KL: *No...no never* .

no never is quietly spoken

TL: *No... not a single time*

Anticipating statement analyst Peter Hyatt, a simple denial — *no* — is more convincing. *Not a single time* is a needless effort to persuade. I think here the caretakers show they are poorly equipped to play acting roles.

I note that at time stamp [25:22] in the background we see the ET ironwork on the fence or gateway. It displays an iconic grey alien image. This iconography occurs all over the ranch. Of course what one puts on one's property is one's own business, but it seems like a way of subtly influencing viewers' expectations of what will be experienced.

TL *You know, that area is interesting because they congregate there and that's also where, you know, there were some reported cow mutilations, and so we been studying that area and we have cameras down there...*

You know is what statement analysts call a need to convince.

KL always seems a little uncomfortable on camera; possibly because she knows she is being used to deceive. I notice to the side that JM is wearing his trademark waistcoat, and obviously his uniform for the program. JM seems to possess a gravity about him that is not solely attributable to his girth. I do wonder whether JM is some sort of on-set enforcer or director.

TT says his digital compass is 90 degrees out at timestamp [27:02], but based on his actual orientation, it seems right to me. We should note by the direction of the shadow, TT's hand makes on his body at timestamp [26:56], he is facing roughly SW or SSW. His app shows 262 degrees west and points his phone outwards to his right. This is consistent with both the way he stands and what is shown, but not with what he asserts. His app is just showing that it is being angled towards the west; nothing else. His assertion is nonsense; he is not reporting what he is actually seeing.

At timestamp [27:05] – the time is 2:36 pm – the shadow will be roughly SSW running to NNE

BA with his analogue compass timestamp [27:18] says north is in a direction that is inconsistent with the shadow direction; visible on the ground as well as of right arm across his left arm.

The direction he says is north, is actually roughly ESE. The mesa to which his back faces obliquely, is to the north. From the compass needle we can see it pointing towards the mesa – it is pointing north and not 190 degrees out as BA asserts. His observation is nonsense. But if you believe someone who was once a Mormon missionary is now being truthful, I have a bridge to sell you...

The intentional misreading of compasses took place before as well. It seems when he said the drilling was affecting the compass, TT was pointing his phone compass at the drill. He then read his position as deviation from north — the mesa — as a magnetic anomaly. It was all just about the direction he pointed his phone in .

The misleading compass farce owes something to not explain how the compass works plus only momentarily showing the instruments. And they would have got away with it too if wasn't for those pesky ~~kids~~ slow motion playbacks and freezes.

The next page shows the compass app in TT's hand at a timestamp of [26.56], shown for about a second at most. The page after shows BA's analogue compass at a timestamp [27.20]. We see this for longer. The reader is invited to check these two orientations to corroborate my assertions, and listen to what these jokers actually say.

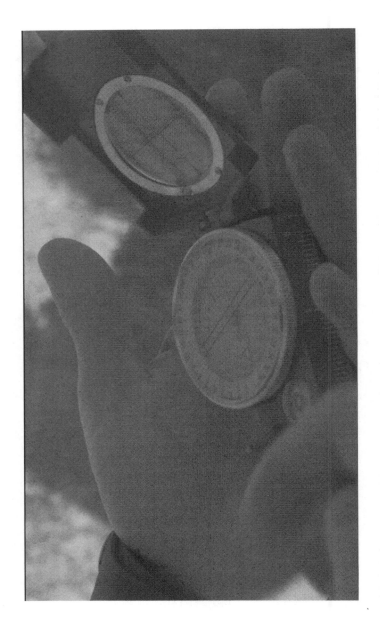

***

They reconvene outside at the Command Center, and review the past events. This final episode of season two, more than anything, demonstrated the Skinwalker *experts* are liars.

TT starts to lecture about asteroid impacts. He invokes ancient astronauts BS about the Book of Ezekiel and an asteroid-meteorite strike on Iraq – formerly ancient Babylon. This isn't even worth deconstructing, but will no doubt gratefully be entertained by shows' groupies.

They kick the subject around a bit. What strikes me though is that no one ever seems to talk over the other as in real life, where one party might give way to the other. There is an orderly exchange of views that always seems to include as many people as possible. I originally cut them slack for scripting, but the degree over the weeks has been ridiculous.

They move onto to what comes next for the investigation

BF: *We have to ask ourselves, what can of worms, what portal are we opening...*

TT: *My personal opinion is that fortune favours the bold...*

EB: *That's right...*

JM: *Yeah, absolutely*

This is exactly what the fandom want to hear of course.

BF asks what the team proposes for the future. TT proposes a blimp to be in the air for a long time. BF says he wants to engage the intelligence community who have been involved in *monitoring our planet*

Why would BF have intelligence links?

BF: *I...I don't believe for one second that a*

lot of what we we're observing here has gone unnoticed. I think we truly are sitting at this table, pioneers; at a time when we see the emerging private space race reaching for the next frontier, you know, planetary exploration.

I think there's good chance that there are areas right here under our own back yard that are worthy of investigation and they could probably provide even more insight into the nature of our universe, and whether we're alone or not.

TT aside: He reprises the Tic Tac video et al...

TT informs the meeting that he is in contact with people with ground penetrating radar that can penetrate up to 2km below the surface.

The program finishes with drone footage of the team all hugging each other on the porch.

Why send up a drone? Isn't eye level sentimentality good enough?

The program and series finishes with TT getting into his car — still in his shirt uniform — and riding into — actually away from — the sunset with BA, TW, and EB in the foreground — like an old time western, and one can see how the sentimentality is being stoked up to make the fans water at the mouth for the next season.

BF ends by saying how they will take the *public along with us,* as TT's car travels away from Skinwalker Ranch...

1/ 5G interference with navigation systems
https://verticalmag.com/news/aviation-experts-warn-5g-rollout-could-result-in-wildly-wrong-altimeter-readings/

2/ Book cover with top to bottom blue filtering applied to the photo, accentuating the white lettering.
https://www.amazon.co.uk/dp/B08KWBLHM2

APPENDIX A – MAPS, PHOTOS, AND SHADOWS

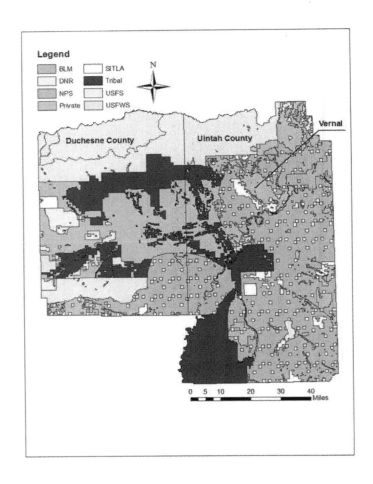

The map on the last page is the general area of the Uintah Basin, courtesy of the website linked underneath:[1]

The key needs some explanation:

BLM = Bureau of Land Management – (I was relieved when I found out this was it stood for. I know *Black Lives Matter* aka *Building Large Mansions* have embezzled donors funds to buy property...but... ah well....)

DNR = Department of Natural Resources

NPS = National Park Service

Private = self-explanatory

SITLA = (Utah) School And Institutional Trust Land Administration

Tribal = self-explanatory

USFS = US Forest Service

USFWS = US Fish and Wildlife Service

I refer the reader to the referenced link and a more useful colour map. Skinwalker Ranch is in the west of Uintah County, bordered by tribal and private areas. To the west of Uintah County is Duchesne County; to the north Daggett County; and to the south Grand County. Salt Lake City, Summit County is where BF flies from in his chopper; this is to the north of Duchesne County.

And for what it's worth, Summit and Grand Counties were the only ones voting for Biden in 2020. That the election was rigged is beyond the remit of this book. No doubt some tourism in the general area might point to prosperity and possibly lessen the Democrat hold, although the appreciation of land prices can benefit a few at the expense of the many.

Once again, a detour into detailed political economy survey is beyond the remit of this book. As in the UK, the US has a twin party dictatorship of corrupt and bribed puppets. Democrats play Tweedledee to the Republicans Tweedledum. Here is a link to the 2020 electoral map of Utah.[2]

For some reason Google Earth gives *Skinwalker Ranch* as further north than the Command Center and the Homesteads.

Here are the coordinates of the one Google Earth is currently carrying for what it calls *Skinwalker Ranch*: latitude 40°24'31.48"N and longitude 109°53'4.80"W In any case, using the Google Earth ruler tool, we can estimate that the northern ranch is roughly ten and a half miles to the north. So please download and install Google Earth if you haven't already got it, and put in those coordinates to see for yourself.

If we go to Homestead Two and zoom in, we soon see the *Skinwalker Ranch* — aka the Sherman-Bigelow-Adamantium Holdings-Fugal Ranch — we are interested in. The coordinates of Homestead Two are latitude 40°15'25.88"N and longitude 109°54'6.31"W

Before zooming out, we can see the mesa to the north, the road running parallel to the famous Triangle Area to the east; basically, three dirt tracks forming an approximate equilateral triangle.

Now zoom out and observe *Skinwalker Ranch Command Center*, approximately ¾ mile to the east of Homestead Two, the *UFO Valley Campground and UTV Tours* to the north west of Homestead Two, and the *Space Wolf Research* to the south.

***

UFOs — or UAPs as the trendy folk are now calling them — have been fairly native to the US south western states since WWII. No surprise given the amount of deserted areas. I have documented the terrestrial origins of UFOs in my other writing, but it's not a popular dream busting analysis that some people want to hear about. Suffice to say, the *UFO Valley Campground* are not allowed to mention *Skinwalker Ranch* in their publicity material. Their website carries the following:[3]

> *Travel up the Mesa & view the area surrounding a famous paranormal hotspot like never before.*

> *Are you brave enough to spend the night 1500 yards from the ranch we can't name due to trademarks and a cease-and-desist order?*

> *As beautiful as it is spooky. Check us out!*

> *All about the people crazy enough to live here!*

Their website carries the following, informing us that campers and tents cost $40 dollars a night.

Meanwhile, *Space Wolf Research* below, leveraging the same initials as *Skinwalker Ranch* carries this:

> *Overnight stay at Space Wolf Research*

> *Volunteer/donate $100 at Space Wolf Research and an overnight stay as one of four individuals to be the first four to be on property.*

About this event

The first four on property at space wolf research one male one female and one couple. This is a research project which requires a $100 donation and volunteer work including one evening Saturday in the morning of Sunday. We accept Venmo or PayPal. Personal message me at ryanpatrickburns@gmail with any questions.[4] And their Facebook page is here.[5]

UFO Valley Campground and *Space Wolf Research* are just riding on the coat tails of Skinwalker Ranch and Uintah Basin lore. I like the idea that people who stay can imagine themselves as *researchers* and donate towards the *research*. I suppose we shall have to wait a few years before we have can have an Arnold Schwarzenegger *Total Recall* memory implanted adventure to Mars – for now we need to use our imaginations....

If you are still in Google Earth, scroll north over *Bottle Hollow Reservoir*. I was thinking some sort of water monster would be appealing for tourism, but no – *stop press there is;* the reader can check this out for themselves.

The reservoir does appear on *10 Most Haunted Campgrounds in Utah*.[6]

Located in ancient Ute Indian territory, this beautiful reservoir lake is great for fishing, hiking, and getting your pants scared off.

A hunting party of Ute Indians frequent the haunted campgrounds.

One is a bit older than the other three, and they're unremarkable other than their strange choice of dress.

When seen, the group is invariably wearing the furs and feathers of a bygone time.

They sit around a fire, motionless and silent.

They're also quite dead.

One group of campers tell of their encounter with the hunting party.

The campers walked right up to the Ute and tried repeatedly to engage them in conversation.

No response.

Even trying a few words in their own language, the campers felt like they were simply being ignored.

It wasn't until a few minutes later when the Indians faded out of view right before their eyes that the campers realized the truth.

The fire crackled for a few more seconds, then disappeared as well.

There was no sign of any burned tinder, or any other evidence that the Ute had been there at all.

***

Moving on to *Skinwalker Ranch Command Center,* I want to get closer, and present some photos of the surrounding area; with specific reference to the last episode of series two. For me, everything was coming together for me after this.

The date of the picture below is of June 19 2015; there was no helicopter landing pad back then. OK, no big deal. Using Google Earth one can find a current picture by going into *View* and then using the displayed slider in the top left corner to get the most current picture. The picture on the page after, dated November 11th, 2021, shows the helipad.

The main point I want to draw readers'
attention to is that the top edge of the helipad is
roughly facing north. This helps our orientation. The
next picture is a shot of BF supposedly landing at
2.07 PM. We will be discussing shadows; this will be
an aid to get a feeling for direction when they
perform the scenario of the *compasses not working*.
I will refer readers back from that episode to this
analysis as an aid.

The reader may be aided in their orientation by turning the picture upside down — with respect to the text on it — angled at about 30 degrees from the horizontal, and lining up the helipad edge so the path from it is in the two o'clock position, and the helipad edge is parallel to the *up* position.

The shadow of the helicopter shows the sun is lying approximately ESE to WNW. If the 2:07 PM time stamp was correct, the shadow should be on the other side, lying approximately SSW to NNE.

If the reader want to check the last episode of series two with the timestamp of [17:36] min, we see a ground level shot of BF leaving the helicopter walking towards the north east pathway to the porch area. We can see from his own longish shadow that it is consistent with the shadow direction of the image given.

At this point I wonder whether any of my readers are familiar with the shadows analysis and the moon landing hoax. The perfect crime, it is said, is very difficult to commit...I wonder what TT has to say about the Apollo hoax given his association with NASA? Not much, I bet...

OK, *big deal,* some might say, *they have used stock footage* for the filming of *The Curse Of Skinwalker Ranch.* But I believe the possibility of having BF already on the ranch and filming from another room, while *deciding the next course of action,* may use the ruse of *flying him in the next day or later* complements the consistent use of the same uniforms worn by the players.

In other words, they can say action that took place over two days, took place over one day. After all, we all know after BF has expressed reluctance about the *next experiment,* it always goes ahead anyway. It's likely the omission of exact dates from series two is an effort to deter nosey parker investigators like myself. If they were straight, why not give the dates when events occurred. Perhaps some business associate of BFs might have watched a programme from series one, noticed the date stamp and said something like, *hey, wait a minute I was having an interview with BF on that date.*

If they tell lies about small things, why not lie about the big things as well. Isn't science supposed to be precise?

Incidentally, the path from where BA escorts BF when he leave the helicopter leads to the narrow south side of the porch where their often look out westward when something surprising *just happens* after a particular talk or discussion is coming to an end. That BA escorts BF all of fifteen or twenty yards is also comical – are they expecting him to be attacked by a skinwalker?

To get our bearings further: to the west and southwest is the *East Field*; east of course in respect of a field to its west. The reader should make themselves familiar with directions and bearing of the various building and features of *Skinwalker Ranch*. So in series two, episode nine when they are looking westwards after the cows have stampeded, the players line up on the western rail of the helicopter enclosure. The direction of the shadows and knowledge that the mesa is to the north blows apart BA's and TT's BS about compasses going wrong. But for that analysis, please read episode ten series two.

1/Uintah Basin – General Land Ownership
https://www.researchgate.net/figure/Land-Ownership-in-the-Uintah-Basin-Source-Utah-State-Geographic-Information-Database_fig8_266486138

2/ 2020 Political Map of Utah
https://www.politico.com/2020-election/results/utah/

3/ UFO Valley Playground
https://www.ufovalleycampground.com/

4/ Space Wolf Research
https://www.eventbrite.com/e/overnight-stay-at-space-wolf-research-tickets-66953637131

5/ Space Wolf Research Facebook page
https://www.facebook.com/spacewolfresearch/posts/the-new-look-for-space-wolf-research-the-unveiling-of-what-it-really-is-image-cr/2640997932596682/

6/ 10 Most Haunted Campgrounds in Utah
https://backpackerverse.com/haunted-campgrounds-utah/

APPENDIX B – THE CAST OF PLAYERS

BACKGROUND

Just as Shaggy always wears his green shirt, Freddy his cravat, Velma her orange sweater, and Daphne her purple dress, the Skinwalker Ranch guys also have their own *Mystery Incorporated* style costumes. The uniforms allow the film producers to obfuscate times frames. They can say the *next day* in the subtitles when in fact it might be the *same day*. This is also aided in series two by the omission of dates in the subtitles.

Along with the outer apparel, a franchise needs certain mannerisms, predispositions, and recurring soap opera like interactions that audiences will recognise and endearingly relate to. Skinwalker Ranch's own *Mystery Inc* have this in spades. The confluence of soap opera and pseudo non-fiction does nothing to upset the suspension of disbelief of the show's fans.

One expects this readiness to believe fills a religious like need that may owe something to the dull uneventful tedious lives that the show provides fans refuge from. I want to now examine the show's main players.

TRAVIS TAYLOR, TT

TT'S UNIFORM IS AN INDIGO SHIRT AND LIGHT BROWN TROUSERS. But he does wear a black shirt for indoor shots of him reflecting on ranch events or *moonlighting(?)* away from Brandon Fugal's *employment(?)*, with the same backdrop for other *Prometheus Entertainment* productions such as *Ancient Aliens* and *The Unexplained with William Shatner* ...

TT is the intentional alpha male of *The Curse Of Skinwalker Ranch*. He is brought in and lauded at the start of series one as the guy who will uncrack the mystery. Hitherto, Erik Bard, EB — *Principal Scientific Investigator* — would necessarily have been undisputed *leader* — whatever that means. The juxtaposition of the two *scientists*, I will leave for when discussing EB, who as far as I know is not interviewed by anyone for any other subject than what is related to *Skinwalker Ranch*.

The University of Alabama in Huntsville where TT collected four of his degrees, including two PhDs — who needs two PhDs!? — also has connections to Robert Bigelow. That Bigelow was into real estate — like Brandon Fugal — sets up an interesting *Triangle Area* of its own...

Who exactly is Travis Taylor, is one of the most interesting questions one can ask about the show. Let's look at most of his Wikipedia entry as of June 2022.[1] I will underline the Wikipedia entries that stand out for me. My additional comments will be in non-italics:

Appendix B – The Cast Of Players

Travis Shane Taylor (born 24 July 1968 in Decatur, Alabama) is an <u>aerospace engineer, optical scientist, science fiction author, and star of National Geographic Channel's Rocket City Rednecks</u>. Taylor has written more than <u>25 technical papers, 14 science fiction novels and two textbooks, and has appeared in multiple television documentaries, including NGC's When Aliens Attack.</u>

Personal biography

    Taylor grew up in rural North Alabama alongside his older brother Gregory, a chief master sergeant of the Air Force Reserves. As a boy, Taylor read science fiction and dismantled household electronics. His father, Charles Taylor, worked as a machinist at Wyle Laboratories, which subcontracted for National Aeronautics and Space Administration (NASA) in the 1960s, wherein he built America's first satellites directly with Wernher von Braun.

    While in high school, Taylor's family moved to Somerville, near Huntsville, next door to an Army scientist. <u>At 17 years old, with the help of his neighbor, he built a radio telescope that won the state science fair and placed sixth in the nation. This led the Army to offer Taylor a job working at Redstone Arsenal on direct energy weapons systems directly out of high school as well as a scholarship. Taylor is a black belt martial artist, a private pilot, a scuba diver, races mountain bikes, competed in triathlons, and has been the lead singer and rhythm guitarist of several hard rock bands</u>. Taylor lives near Huntsville with his wife Karen, daughter Kalista Jade, two dogs Stevie and Wesker, and his cat Kuro.

He is more credentialled than both James Bond and Jeff Goldblum's scientist character in *Independence Day* put together. On first examination it is very difficult to believe the sum total of his achievements is anything more than narrative building. On reflection though, it seems to me that TT is trying to *become a scientist*; he is building his own narrative of himself We all do this to some extent, but after a while TT's academic career must surely be regarded as narcisstic certification collecting exercise?

An earlier suspicion was that he was some sort of hybrid actor-intelligence asset. I tend to think TT is someone who has acted out in life what he thinks a *scientist should be like*. He has studied the role without really assuming the questioning mind of what an investigator should really have. Wearing the apparel of archbishop doesn't make a man spiritual. And indeed, the fact that he is fabricator of untruths undoes whatever worth his paper qualifications signify to those impressed by the fool's gold he continually offers up.

Education

Taylor's degrees are from <u>Auburn University (B.E.E. '91), University of Western Sydney (MS '04), and the University of Alabama, Huntsville (MS '94, Ph.D. '99, MSE '01, Ph.D. '12). He has a doctorate in optical science and engineering, a master's degree in physics, a master's degree in aerospace engineering, a master's degree in astronomy, and a bachelor's degree in electrical engineering.</u>

With all that effort to jump through hoops, how can he know anything substantial? Are six degrees a sign of intelligence, affluence, ignorance or what? Who can afford to study for six degrees? What do six degrees afford anyone except adulation of people of a religious disposition and a misdirected need to prove something to the world?

Bibliography

According to Taylor, after he expressed his dissatisfaction with space opera and the comparative dearth of recent hard science fiction, he was challenged by his wife to write his first book, and studied Robert A. Heinlein's works for stylistic influence.

I will let the reader view his science fiction writing entry listed in Wikipedia, but I'll just include one snippet:

In the sequel, The Tau Ceti Agenda, the Separatist movement prepares a strike against Earth governments. The plan: Kill the U.S. president at Disney World and drive a quantum-teleported kamikaze starship into a heavily populated city.

One thing the fanatical Separatists haven't figured on: an America military unleashed by a fighting president: an ex-Marine determined that terrorists won't have the final word on humanity's future! Sequel to One Day on Mars. Published 5/1/2008.

This sounds similar to the narrative of *Independence Day*. I note that from TT's sci fi, he invests the same standing in elected officials as being legitimate leaders as the mainstream would want us to believe of real life politicians. This reprises his own fascination with the *importance of appearance*. During the early episodes I was struck by two distinct possibilities regarding TT: either he was a very accomplished but very naive individual, or a phony.

By the end of series two, I was convinced of the latter, notwithstanding he is someone who has jumped through the hoops to be recognised. His TV series *Rocket City Rednecks* uses a term that is sometimes regarded as offensive to working class provincial types of people. It is akin in this usage as Black people calling themselves *niggers* – seeking pride in the appropriation of the derogatory. Naturally, working class people from the southern USA might wish to bask in this inverted snobbery. That many people from Alabama may identify with TT just because of his origins does illustrate the pitfalls of identifying with someone just because they originate from the same place or group.

TT might have had some deep down need to prove himself, showcasing his intelligence — albeit it credentialled by examination bodies — alongside his *good ole boy* roots; notwithstanding he is as much a con artist as the more aristocratic Brandon Fugal. The social class aspect of TT's character will not be so evident to non-American viewers as natives in my opinion. The elevation of a working-class hero is an important part of TT veneration for many; the producers are giving the audience what they want.

Whoever TT *really is*, his sci fi work and television work indicates the sort of *scientist* he keeps referring to himself as, is the constructed media portrayal of one that seeks deference from a gullible public. The cult of *scientism* as opposed to genuine science seeks to appoint high priests of knowledge who *only fools* — such as we cynics — would dare to contradict.

Moving on from Wikipedia, we hear that on April 22 2022:[2]

Radiance Technologies Appoints TV Personality Dr. Travis S. Taylor as a Principal

Research Scientist; CEO Bill Bailey Quoted

Radiance Technologies announced on Friday that Dr. Travis S. Taylor, scientist, author, engineer and television star, has joined the company as a principal research scientist.

"Dr. Taylor is an outstanding and highly qualified scientist whose inventive way of thinking will be a great asset for Radiance," said Radiance Technologies CEO Bill Bailey.

In his new role, Dr. Travis Taylor will be support technical activities across the company as part of Radiance's defense sector. With more than 20 years of experience supporting NASA, the U.S. Army Space and Missile Defense Command as well as other customers, Dr. Taylor brings a wealth of experience to the company, which includes advanced concepts in space technologies.

In addition, he's also starred in television shows such as the National Geographic Channel's "Rocket City Rednecks" and the History Channel's "The Secret of Skinwalker Ranch." Taylor has also written two textbooks, over 15 papers and 21 science fiction novels.

"I'm a hands-on type of researcher, and I really look forward to getting acquainted with all the work being done at Radiance and what we might do that is new in the future," said Taylor.

I believe that TT has been so busy getting degree, writing books, and obtaining black belts in karate that his need to affirm he is an *hands-on type of researcher* is far from the truth. TT's appointment is a public relations exercise in the same way the appointments of *Shaggy* and *Scooby* to a university's paranormal department would be.

***

As well as appearing on *The Curse Of Skinwalker Ranch*, TT is a regular journeyman of other programmes within the *History Channel/Prometheus Entertainment/A&T* stable of *Ancient Aliens* and related mystery genre. I'm of no doubt he is an intelligent man, but that he appears to give expert testimony on diverse phenomena not within the compass of his half a dozen degrees, indicates that TT, *the expert scientist*, is a script reading extra for pseudo non-fiction documentaries for the most part.

The word *scientist* is too broad a meaning to worthy of any usage in my opinion. Someone who has a sociology degree may be described as a *scientist*. Does that mean they can pontificate on something like the Big Bang theory for example?

More worryingly in current times are doctors who are paid very high salaries to prostitute themselves to Big Pharma by claiming vaccines are safe while knowing nothing; they just parrot what is expected of them like a *Prometheus Entertainment* employee. I find TT relatively innocent compared to publicly funded scientists and experts in terms of the deception they are involved with. My take on him is hard, but I bare him no malice; there are far more people masquerading under the cloak of scientism who are doing far more harm than TT is.

***

Here in a *Prometheus Entertainment* production of *The Unexplained, The Underground World,* series 1, episode 21, hosted by William Shatner, we see TT giving lie to the notion he is a kind of Hollywood science fiction scientist *who knows everything.* I have collected what he has said from this episode, and put in some commentary. The subject of the discussion is the *Cheyenne Mountain Complex* that will be familiar to watchers of the *Stargate* science fiction series:

Here is TT giving his two cents:

The Cheyenne Mountain Complex was built err in the sixties and was operational in 1967, and the idea was that you have all your information for our national missile defence and offence capabilities to be operated from there. So, it had to be able to withstand major natural and manmade disasters such as nuclear attack. So, the airforce and army and navy; all the services; they were in there. Basically, it was the nexus of our cold war defence centre.

I have no problem with TT reading a script or engaged in some prior swotting to deliver this, but isn't this what a news presenter does? If he is a news presenter for this then any delivery of information not covered by his six degrees means he is extending the idea of *scientist* into the realm of the general *know-it-all* beloved of Hollywood science fiction heroes. Another piece in the episode features TTs delivering information on geology; *The Cave of Crystals* in Mexico:[3]

It's amazing. There are crystal that are huge; so big that you can walk across em, and for this crystals to have gotten as big as they are, they have to have been growing for hundreds of thousands of years....

It's 90 to 100 percent relative humidity in this cave, and it's always over 100 F . You might think, well 113 degrees isn't that bad; it gets 140 degrees in the deserts of Iraq all the time, and people live there. But the relative humidity in those deserts is 10 percent. In this cave there's so much humidity you can't sweat and cool your body off...

And speaking of a worker who unwisely stayed too long in the cave TT adds some *sense of mystery* to this death, says:

Now, it's unclear if he died from the air quality, the heat, the humidity, or could it have been the extremophile microorganisms that were in there?

It's interesting that while TT extols the scientific method and uses his, *speaking as a scientist,* mantra frequently, he will speculate about anything with little proof. His equating the *Book of Ezekiel* and meteorites in the last episode of series two of *The Curse Of Skinwalker Ranch* for example, demonstrates his ability to walk the high wire of scientism and assorted ancient alien BS.

And in this same episode of the Shatner series, TT displays knowledge of oceanography, anthropology, and the *hollow earth mythology* fallaciously attached to Admiral Byrd. The whole Admiral Byrd supposed entry into a *hollow earth* in 1947 is ridiculous but will be interesting to many of my readers. [4,5]

There's water on the surface in huge oceans. What if there's a hole in the mantle that allows some of it to drain somewhere. Did it get captured there when the earth was created in its formation? To give you an example, in "Mammoth Cave" in Kentucky there were the remains of a shark from 330 million years ago. And this sea creature found in cave; in a cave! Not in an ocean but in a cave! What if this cave was part of an ocean system that went deeper underground?

TT should know this is nonsense. Sea levels have risen and fallen over millions of years. Cataclysmic floods being associated with the end of ice-ages is an uncontroversial idea, but TT *gets with the programme* and voices the a tenuous idea, necessary for continuity of progressing the mysterious programme narrative, and playing on the ignorance of many viewers, to claim it is because of an underground ocean. How can you constantly vocalise as *a scientist* when you know that you tell lies?

Just after that another guy speaking, starts off, *as a scientist*. It's just another variant of the newspaper headline beginning, *experts say*, isn't it?

TT, however, continues:

The earth is about 7 to 8000 miles in diameter; that's pretty big. We only ever drilled to about 8 miles deep. We have no idea what's at the centre of the earth. You know, we have theories that there's this molten ball iron core spinning around, it's magnetised, whatever, but we really don't know. There could be a completely different world that we just don't understand yet cause we've never been there to do experiments and do science on it and understand what's going on...

The episode is made in 2020, and as the background is the same recognisable out of focus studio setting he swaps his indigo for black shirt in, we may assume he is reading for various other mystery narratives. If BF is funding the research at *Skinwalker Ranch*, he obviously isn't bothered by TT's moonlighting for other projects.

Come to think about it, if TT and the rest were involved in real science, the final film publication would take place after the mystery had been *solved*, after many mundane experiments had been repeatedly been performed; the promotion of a week by week unfolding revelations is about entertainment not scientific enquiry.

You can't have both. Real research must include boring periods of sameness and little novelty. This is certainly not true of *The Curse Of Skinwalker Ranch*.

People want deliverance from their everyday grind when watching TV. There is always something *anomalous* on Skinwalker Ranch; there is always something that TT describes as *crazeee*. By the same token TT is always on the verge of attempting the final explanation of what is going on. This parallels the expectations of those expecting disclosure in the UFO religion, and taps into the same yearning as those proclaiming the immediacy of *The Rapture*...

The construct of the all-knowing scientist or expert, validated by corrupt academia, is well loved of an establishment who bedeck their high priests of scientism in the robes of unquestionable narrative. Give someone a PhD, a stethoscope, a white coat, and a film script, and anyone who disagrees with them is a nazi, racist, or a conspiracist terrorist – right?

ERIK BARD, EB
EB'S UNIFORM IS A CREAM SHIRT AND DARK GREY TROUSERS.

EB is billed as the show's principal investigator. Unlike TT, his achievements are underplayed, and he has no Wikipedia entry. He is in relation to TT on the Skinwalker soap opera what Henry McGee is to Benny Hill. TT might have *Astrophysicist* in his screen title, but EB has no *Plasma Physicist* subtitling for his appearances. EB is TT's straight man. It is TT who usually delivers the scientific punch lines.

Here's what the website *Celebs Fortune* says of EB, May 6, 2021:

Appendix B – The Cast Of Players

Erik Christopher Bard is a plasma physicist from Lehi, Utah, known for his role as the principal investigator of the ever-so-mysterious Skinwalker Ranch. Among the many previously unrecognized people involved in running the property, Bard is also brought into the spotlight with The Secret of Skinwalker Ranch, which did quite fine among a handful of viewers.

Like most of the cast members of History Channel's newer reality show, Bard is also quite shy of social media, despite being a man of science and technology. Regardless, there are a few places his works have been recognized throughout his career.

Erik Bard's Resume Is Pretty Intensive and Begins from Well Back in the '90s

Erik Bard enrolled in Transylvania University in the late '80s with a Thomas Jefferson full scholarship in Physics and move on to the University of Kentucky in 1989 two years later, denying the continuation at his former college. While majoring in Physics there (and minoring in mathematics), he immediately started working as a process engineer at IBM until 1993.

After leaving his work at IBM in 1993, Bard mentions in his LinkedIn profile that he went to Eastern Europe during the post-Soviet era for two years before returning to work for Lexmark in 1995 as an associate engineer involved in the printing technology industry. After staying at Lexmark for just about a year, he went back to school at Brigham Young University in 1997 to get his degree in Plasma Physics.

The physicist's area of expertise has a lot to do with charged particles, having already worked for electrophotography R&D at IBM, and his focus at BYU was the unusual behavior in the motion of charged particles confined at cyclotron orbital resonance with the electromagnetic cavity modes of a Penning trap. He got his master's degree in 2002.

While studying at BYU, he was a development and test engineer at PowerStream Technology from March 2000 to August 2003. He moved on as a senior scientist at MOXTEK later in 2003, working with X-ray products. After 5 years at MOXTEK, he was a lead scientist at Millenniata of a group that developed the "M disc" until mid-2010.

Just over a year later, he became the chief science officer at Motion Sciences and kept the job until exactly two years later in 2013. Following the stint, he became an independent physics consultant at CJ's Toybox for a year and then at MicroRay, LLC., for less than a year in 2015. Being the VP of engineering at Brandon Fugal's Axcend Corp. was another one of his short-lived jobs, in the same year Fugal bought the Skinwalker Ranch.

However, his big leap had already come in late 2010 when he joined ML3 Scientific as the director of Applied Physics before taking over as the director of the company itself in May 2012. He still holds his position while working on the Skinwalker Ranch and is listed as the co-founder of the firm. And according to Dun & Bradstreet, their revenue is collected to $96,335 in 2021, at the time of writing.

Bard Has a Dozen Patents to His Name

Erik Bard is also labeled as an inventor on account of the number of patents he's filed under his name and his career track record of working in most R&D departments. And considering his continuous allegiance to the serendipities in

Physics, especially in electrophotography and X-rays during the turn of a technological revolution, there's always something new happening in that part of the world.

According to Justia Patents, the 53-year-old has at least 12 inventions to his name between 2008 and 2013. All of them are partnered with various people he's worked with at Moxtek or Brigham Young University. And the majority of them are in research of X-rays.

Bard's Alumni US profile also lists a plethora of skills under his name, going from technical writing & C++ programming to spectroscopy & nanotechnology. And as a principal investigator at Skinwalker Ranch, he also conducted "a low-profile observational science program" within the compound quite before the History Channel continued it into a show.[6]

I suggest that with respect to a term that is overworked, EB may be the *real scientist* on the show if there is one. Where are TT's patents and inventions? EB was doing real hands on stuff rather than engaging in PhD paper chases.

When I first started to study *The Curse of Skinwalker Ranch*, I entertained the possibility that although there was scripting in place, the rest of the cast were nevertheless being duped by microwave and gamma weaponry, and that EB was the *outside asset* directing various weapons systems. I also briefly entertained the idea that the series might have been some perverted advertisement for weapons systems to be shown among international arms dealers. My thinking was partly based on EB's access to the Command Center and that he experiences no dizzy bouts or radiation burns himself.

As my understanding of the show's modus operandi moved on, EB's immunity from various manifestations of *skinwalker attacks* has become another Sherlock Holmes's dog that didn't bark. While EB often has a contrived looked of *wow* and *earnestness*, I surmise a fake attack against himself is something he wouldn't be able to pull off. For all we know any attempt to *perform* an attack might have just been left on the cutting room floor.

Nevertheless, EB may still be involved in any microwave chicanery or deliberate instrumentation failure. But given the closeness and necessary scripting of the show, whatever is going on must be a teamwide conspiracy.

My understanding of the show as a grift — and theme park development initiative — more than anything more conspiratorial in respect of weapons systems advertising, was a little underwhelming for me. My former hypothesis however, was based on the premise of not believing anything on the TV, and in this I feel vindicated.

JIM SEGALA, JS

JS only appeared in season one. I happened to notice him briefly in a season two flashback. I wondered on occasion if he looked a little disgusted with the whole business, but that is just speculation on my part. Someone posted a message on Reddit:[7]

What happened to the white headed fellow from the first season? He's obviously not on season two. Does anyone know his story or what happened to him.

To which the answer came back:

Dr. Jim Segala. He's an associate professor at a university in Rhode Island if I recall. He's yet another physicist, but seems to have more medical connections to Dr. Eric Bards electronics experience and Dr. Travis Taylor's aerospace and television experience.

He's still listed as associated with the ranch on their official website.

Considering this season was filmed last summer during the height of the Pandemic, he may have preferred to remain home or have other more pressing responsibilities.

You may be able to find him on other social media and ask him, or ask other members of the research team on social media.

JS is a difficult character to find anything about. For example:[8]

How do i go about sending him correspondence? I can't find any social media for him. He has at least one science groupie.. Me! 😊*im sure others would love to comment and ask questions of him. For instance, ,"are you married"?* 😊😊*just kidding. But really, I'm sure people would love interacting with him via social media..*

Most of the Skinwalker cast are male. I'm certainly no arbiter of the male aesthetic but judging from social media comments the cast may have been chosen in part for their attractiveness. In any case, JS may have regretted his association with Skinwalker Ranch.

BRANDON FUGAL, BF
BF'S UNIFORM IS A DARK SUIT, WHITE SHIRT – WITH OR WITHOUT A TIE.

Wearing a suit is a way of *suggesting authority*. The deference shown to BF about whatever next experiment should be performed on

Skinwalker Ranch is a regular soap contrivance. The BF, TT, and BA triangle is a regular round-table meme. For a man in charge BF does not strike me as walking in comfortable shoes. He often seems nervous and apprehensive.

This celebsfortune.com Jul 5 2020 article I reproduce in full, amounts to a mainstream advertising piece for BF. I have underlined certain lines of the italicised article, and intermingled my own comments in upright text. So the reader is hereby invited to literally read between the lines:[9]

Brandon Daniel Fugal

For someone named the "CCIM Utah Agent of the Year" and "2019 Office Broker of the Year" founding and working at the number one commercial real estate firm in the Intermountain West, you know Brandon Fugal is living large. And with his most recent reveal as the owner of the mysterious "Skinwalker Ranch" as well, his status of prominence has folded over, more than before. And sure, it's boosted his net worth that no one exactly knows yet.

Fugal's plan for a career in real estate started when he was in Pleasant Grove High School in Utah and obtained his real estate license at 18. He immediately began his career in the corporate real estate world. <u>With experiences as a senior associate at "Grubb & Ellis/Wallace Associates" and vice president of "Utah Realty Group", he co-founded a business of his own, the Salt Lake City office of "Coldwell Banker Commercial (CBC)" in 1998.</u>

<u>With a stellar, high-flying real estate career that he put CBC on the map, he worked his way into the infamous Skinwalker Ranch, known as the</u>

hotspot for extra-terrestrial activities, and one scientist he associated while there suggested he should be the one to buy the property from Robert Bigelow. Of course, he is a big science geek himself, and he's a more humble person than you can imagine from a real estate magnate.

So, he buys a ranch because a scientist suggests it to him. Hmmm

Why Forbes Hasn't Calculated His Net Worth Yet, Probably

Brandon Daniel Fugal bought the 512-acre "Skinwalker Ranch" in 2016 from aerospace billionaire Robert Bigelow [net worth: $1 billion] in a super-secret deal that no one knew about the new owner. The identity of the owner, that is. Fugal was well-known in his state. And he still doesn't want to reveal how much he paid for the land, but if Forbes askes him to, he might.

Of all the crazy rich people Forbes cover, Fugal should have come under their radar. But there has never even been a mention of his name in a single article from the record-keeping organization, despite there been records of his record-breaking real estate business. It's not like they've not got their hands on some exclusive billionaires with more complicated transaction list already.

So why is Fugal not in Forbes' net worth radar, even after the launch of "The Secret of Skinwalker Ranch" on "History Channel?" For one thing, Fugal decided to come out as the owner of the weird land only as recently as March 2020, when "Vice" wrote a column on him, despite allowing History Channel into his world way before. And for another, Forbes likely calculates people's net worth *on a yearly basis. Come back next year, and we may have a number too.*

Here's the Stretch of His Empire!

"CBC" merged with "Colliers International" in 2018, but don't worry, he's still the chairman of the company. And mind you, he's not limited to real estate only. With a piqued interest in all things science, he's a part of the foundation group of a number of technology-related companies in and around Utah.

He has fingers in many pies – just like TT.

It's pretty obvious co-founding "Coldwell" was the biggest leap of his career. With the success he's got there (along with worldwide recognition also, of course), he's been able to launch a number of other projects and companies into forgery. One of the first companies he co-founded was "Cypher Corporation" in 2010, a Utah-based software startup that developed Neural Network-based binaural++ noise suppression algorithms. He was the principal until it was acquired by "Cirrus Logic Inc." in April 2017.

He later co-founded "Texas Growth Fund IIIC" in early 2016 and has been a board member since. Another technology-related brand he co-founded was "Axcend" that developed nanoflow liquid chromatography (LC) systems in the Provo area of Utah. And quite recently, he's a board member and the strategic advisor of the Corona Virus initiative "Zenerchi LLC", a cross-company in Salt Lake City and Ho Chi Minh City, Vietnam.

I have little time for anyone who gets money from the scamdemic, but that is beyond the remit of this book to deconstruct. And this is the biggest blot by BF's name in my opinion. I can forgive him the Skinwalker Ranch scam.

Additionally, he remains in the Utah Valley University Foundation Board, Utah National Parks Council Executive Board, Utah Valley Chamber of Commerce Board (and co-chair of the Executive Roundtable) and Women's Leadership Institute Board, while being a member of the "Ancient Historical Research Foundation (AHRF)".

He is also the owner of the shell corporation "Adamantium Holdings, LLC", through which he bought the "Skinwalker Ranch" and also the reason you didn't know who the owner was. And not to forget, he has another charity foundation called "Thanksgiving Development."

For British and other readers, *LLC* is the approximate American equivalent of the British *LTD*; that is, a limited liability company. Unlike a PLC, those running a LLC/LTD are more hidden from public scrutiny. We might infer that the movers and shakers behind *Adamantium Holdings, LLC* had intended to make a *documentary* about *Skinwalker Ranch* all along; leveraging the already grifted canon of *Skinwalker Ranch*.

His Multi-Million Dollar Accomplishments Are a Thing of Beauty

During his time at making Salt Lake City's "Coldwell" office number one among 220 offices worldwide, Brandon Fugal was recognized undoubtedly as the #1 agent globally. He's also made Colliers the number one commercial real estate firm in the Intermountain West. His clientele list includes "Charles Schwab & Co, Inc.", "The Northwestern Mutual Life Insurance Company",

"*Novell, Inc.*", and the "*Workers Compensation Fund.*"

With his dominating abilities, he's leased at least a million square feet of properties and closed over 100 prominent transactions every year. He's directed the leasing processes of "The Towers at South Towne", "Parrish Crossing", the "Sandy City Centre", and "Canyon Park Technology Center", among others.

As for the sales, he's accomplished the sale of the "*Cottonwood Corporate Center*" *for* **$100 million,** *the* "*Embassy Suites/Convention Center*" *for* **$100 million,** *the* "*Rare Downtown Development Parcels*" *for* **$10 million** *and* "*Banyan Building*" *for* **$2.2 million.** *If you want the true figure of his sales empire, <u>Brandon Fugal has crafted over</u>* **<u>$6 billion</u>** <u>*in real estate transactions.*</u>

<u>*Due to his recognition, Brandon Fugal has been featured in the "Wall Street Journal", "Money Magazine", "Bloomberg", "Real Estate Forum", "Real Estate Executive Magazine", "Commercial Property News", and "Utah Business". Additionally, Fugal was also featured nationally as one of "Real Estate Forum's Top 40 under Forty" and as well as a "Top National Dealmaker". In May 2020, he was named the "CCIM Utah Agent of the Year" and "Office Broker of the Year".*</u>

No doubt the various *Oscars* of the business world.

He's As Social As He Can Get

And getting to a more fun side of Fugal, he had his own band called **"Supplicant",** *signed to* "*StarPointe Records*". *Can you imagine? There are a few music videos here and there. He also owns a*

"Airbus H130", the helicopter professionally called "Eurocopter EC130" costing around $2.4 million, and a sweet Lamborghini. He's come here after upgrading from Porsche, Jaguar to Mercedes-Benz. With a whole "Aero Dynamic Jets", you know he's living large.

***

Now it, must be said that any mainstream media piece on any subject will have political and monetary reasons for its execution. All truthseekers know this. The mainstream media are owned by the same matrix of business affiliations that will be occupied with politics, technology, real estate, and so on. Teasing out these links can be quite a research undertaking. By the same token, we may see that a mainstream article's intention is to shepherd the majority of its readers to a particular viewpoint. The mainstream media and its affiliates need the propaganda for their purposes. Unfortunately for them, there are unbrainwashed people, they label as *conspiracy theorists*, who can read between the lines. So propaganda can be a two edged sword.

This piece is dates March 10, 2020 , written by M J Banias. Once again, the italicised text are intermingled with mine in upright text:[10] <u>I also underline the more interesting comments.</u>

This Is the Real Estate Magnate Who Bought Skinwalker Ranch, a UFO Hotspot

Brandon Fugal bought the infamous Utah ranch from aerospace billionaire Robert Bigelow in 2016.

The person who owns the infamous Skinwalker Ranch, a supposedly haunted UFO hotspot in Utah, has decided to come out of the shadows.

Twenty-two stories up in a striking glass building in downtown Salt Lake City, I sat down with Brandon Fugal, a Utah-based real estate mogul and tech investor. Overlooking the city's skyline, the 46-year-old business leader pointed out Utah's most famous landmarks: Temple Square, the global headquarters of the Church of Jesus Christ of Latter-day Saints, also known as the Mormons, and only two blocks north of it, Utah's State Capitol Building.

Surrounding these thrones of Church and State, two ideals that are not totally separate in Utah, were half a dozen commercial buildings and skyscrapers that Fugal has represented. Fugal was cofounder and owner of Coldwell Banker Commercial Advisors before it merged with Colliers International. His name seems connected with nearly every commercial real estate deal in the Intermountain West. He is also a tech investor, venture capitalist and entrepreneur.

"You can ask me anything, and I'll tell you the truth," he said, turning away from the window.

He sat down at a long table. I immediately asked him the question I had been waiting to ask since I boarded my flight to Utah.

"Why the hell did you buy Skinwalker Ranch? Are you crazy?" I asked.

He burst out laughing. "Maybe a little?"

The ranch, a 512 acre property in Utah's Uintah Basin, is known for being a hotspot of UFO sightings and paranormal stories. In 2016, aerospace billionaire Robert Bigelow sold the ranch to Fugal, though his identity has remained a secret until now.

In November, Fugal invited me to see the ranch, which he has overhauled with new sensors and cameras designed to detect UFOs or other abnormalities. At the time, he would only allow me to come if I promised to keep him anonymous in that initial story, however, he has since agreed for his identity to be revealed for the purpose of this interview.

"Why does someone like you buy something like Skinwalker Ranch?," I asked.

"You're right. It is strange. Skinwalker Ranch, as a project, is so unconventional and so outside of my normal course of business and really, frankly, anyone's normal course of business, that it presents a whole new problem set," he said.

"*I've lost some sleep over it. I worry about what some of my clients and colleagues will think. It's controversial. That is why I've waited so long and stayed out of the spotlight.*"

Fugal said that he knew he could not keep his ownership of the ranch secret forever. After all, it is one of the most scientifically studied paranormal hotspots on the planet. He recognizes that given the high profile nature and notoriety of the place, he would have to eventually engage with the press and the public.

And so the narrative of the owner reluctant to enter the public domain continues. In truth, publicity is exactly what the development of a theme park needs.

Recently, the ranch was the subject of a broader Defense Intelligence Agency study, known as the Advanced Aerospace Weapons System Applications Program or AAWSAP. According to an article in The New York Times, in 2007, a Defense Intelligence Agency official visited the ranch, and a short time later, met with Senator Harry Reid of Nevada. "Mr. Reid said he met with

[DIA] agency officials shortly after his meeting with Mr. Bigelow and learned that they wanted to start a research program on UFOs." Bigelow was given a government contract and his company received $22 million to study and generate reports on exotic science, UFOs, and other anomalous phenomena. The strange events on the ranch, as well as other locations bearing purported paranormal anomalies, were involved in the study. <u>AAWSAP was cancelled after two years and, in 2011, Bigelow's government funding ran out.</u>

Are we expected that what Bigelow couldn't find out with $22 million at his command could be discovered by BF and the rest of a Television cast? It bears repeating that the government are hardly likely to let go of an asset like *Skinwalker Ranch* if the phenomena are genuine.

Fugal is a science fiction geek. He has a large movie memorabilia collection, complete with the shot-up jacket Arnold Schwarzenegger wore in "The Terminator" and the black robe Marlon Brando wore in "Superman The Movie" when he sentenced General Zod to an eternity in Krypton's interdimensional prison system. He told me that he's always had a nerdy passion for science, and while his real estate empire and brokerage operations are firmly rooted to the ground with cement and bricks, he is always daydreaming about future possibilities in technology and physics.

I believe *The Curse of Skinwalker Ranch* is more of an advertisement for the realisation of real estate appreciation than a grift it has been relegated as. The programme is selling a dream that increased tourism will realise. To call the series a *grift* is to belittle the supervillain aspirations of BF. It is not of the same scope of villainy that Lex Luther planned by detonating a nuke and so increasing his real estate purchases by creating new seafront properties, but *The Curse Of Skinwalker Ranch* should be respected as part of a scam rather than just a grift based on garnering TV revenues.

Fugal's journey to Skinwalker Ranch began in 2010. He and several other investors launched a project focused on testing gravitational physics theories involving exotic propulsion and renewable energy. In really simple terms, it was an attempt to create a gravitational reduction device that could produce clean energy. Fugal admits it was a shot in the dark.

"It was a challenging time. Admittedly, we were all governed by this childlike wonder. We were filled with excitement and gut-wrenching frustration at every turn," Fugal said.

"To be blunt, there were issues concerning the original partner involved with the project. None of us anticipated the emotional or technical difficulties involved," he added. "We made changes to the team, forged ahead, but in the end, we all knew it was a big risk. Not every bet pays off."

This is interesting if true. I'm sure the deep state already possesses antigravity technology. If BF's team had been able to carry through this project it would probably have been sabotaged; notwithstanding that sabotage or dissuasion could have happened anyway. Any device that produces cheap energy will run afoul of the status quo who would dislike the upsetting of the petrodollar applecart. I go into this topics in *Fake Aliens And The Phony Nuke World Order.*

Fugal continued to invest in and launch other technology companies. From various software ventures to most recently a company that has developed a shoebox-sized high-performance liquid chromatograph that enables immediate analysis of various liquids such as blood.

"It's James Bond/Mission Impossible tech," Fugal explained with a grin.

Though Fugal's pursuit of breakthroughs in advanced physics was not a success, there was a silver lining. Several scientists who were brought in to consult on the project, namely Dr. Hal Puthoff and Dr. Christopher Green, were also involved in Bigelow's DIA project. They became friends. Even after the project was shut down in 2014, Fugal stayed in touch with these scientists.

"They wanted to introduce me to Mr. Bigelow because of the positive experience we had working together and asked if I would be willing to potentially entertain meeting with Mr. Bigelow regarding the ranch," Fugal stated. "I had heard of the ranch but I never really thought about it until they proposed the idea."

Fugal traveled to Las Vegas to meet with Bigelow and they spent a day together talking about various topics, from Bigelow's personal interest in the paranormal to their entrepreneurial projects to space exploration.

I find it strange that BF while sharing RB's interest in real estate is connected to him via scientists. Did they know each other before, and the introduction via the scientists is just a ruse? This is just speculation on my part. Also, observe the delight in experiencing a supervillain lair.

"It was an absolute honor to meet Mr. Bigelow," Fugal said. "Say what you want about his beliefs and his practices, he is a very intriguing fellow. *I consider him a friend*, and Bigelow

Aerospace reminded me of a James Bond villain lair. Very cool."

BF's relationship seems to be a little ambivalent. In the TV show, BF has referred to RB as Bob Bigelow — *indicating friendship* — Mr Bigelow — *indicating respect* — and Bigelow — *indicating exasperation at the supposed classification of RB's findings.* If this *classification* is for reasons of national defence, why hasn't the government acquired the ranch, and if BF and RB are genuine friends, then why the secrecy. To use one of TT's catchphrases, *it's crazeee...*

The sale was arranged, Fugal flew in on his private helicopter and assessed the property, and purchased Skinwalker Ranch following months of legal negotiations. Fugal believes that he was the ideal successor. With a background in commercial real estate development and a passion for science, he also lives and works in Utah.

"The important scientific mission aside, the ranch provides an escape for me from my daily work," Fugal said.

Fugal participated in The Secret of Skinwalker Ranch, a History channel documentary that will premiere March 31. He declined to say how much he paid for the ranch. The following is a Q&A I had with him, it has been edited for length and clarity:

Motherboard: Are you susceptible to magical thinking?
Fugal:

History has long forgotten the names of the men and women who told the Wright brothers that they would never build a working airplane. We do remember the two men who suffered from magical thinking however. Necessity is the mother of invention, but sometimes crazy ideas also play their part.

Do you think you will make history?

We are all judged by it in the end. I honestly don't know, but I do believe this project has significant scientific value.

Do you believe in aliens?

[Laughs] Science and discovery are what drive me. It's not money. It's not that I'm obsessed with UFOs or little green men or cattle mutilations or shape-shifting demonic entities. I have no idea if aliens exist. You'd have to ask them.

People have speculated that you are trying to develop a 'paranormal retreat' or a tourist destination.

Really? That isn't going to happen. The ranch isn't some place for ghost hunters to get their jollies. It's a serious scientific endeavor that requires patience and humility, and I have committed significant resources dedicated to discovering the truth of what is really happening. What a silly idea.

There is zero intention to monetize it in any way, although we do have traditional ranching activities such as raising cattle.

This is brilliant question. I do not believe his answer. In fact there are several other operations grifting on the back of Skinwalker Ranch in the area who are not allowed to even mention *Skinwalker Ranch* in their advertising material. That the area could be a competitor to the Roswell UFO industry is certainly something a real estate operator might have an interest in promoting. That it is fenced off, serves the purposes of a pseudo *Area 51-Roswell* attraction.

And the upcoming History TV show? Is there a financial stake in it for you?

I have yet to personally take a penny related to my involvement with the show. The show is primarily a vehicle to inform the public regarding the reality of what we are monitoring and recording on the ranch. I believe it is the greatest science project of our time. I want to be clear. The ranch has been hidden from the public for a long time. The TV show presents an opportunity to allow the public some access and view of what is truly occurring there. I can't just open the gates. That would be irresponsible.

There are more ways than making money than directly from the show. The value of the land around the area might give a capital increase to anyone who holds it.

How about the local indigenous groups? Have they been involved in the process?

We have been working closely with the Native American elders since acquiring the property, as well as reaching out to tribal leaders in the spirit of friendship and collaboration. We are focused on science, but there may be historical and cultural aspects related to the property that we will need to carefully consider and study in the future. One of our full-time caretakers is a credentialed and published anthropologist, which I think underscores the fact that we are committed to the history of the property and area. I have nothing but the utmost respect for the land and the tribes that surround it.

What do you think it is? Have you had any strange experiences on the ranch itself?

I have no idea. Perhaps it's an intelligence from another reality or dimension. Perhaps it is some unknown natural phenomenon. I'm open to many possibilities. My personal beliefs here don't really matter. What does the data say? That is all that matters. Currently, we have evidence for anomalous injuries, footage of anomalous aerial phenomena, transient EMF and a whole array of other bizarre things. As for your second question, a shockingly high number of people who I consider 'normal' have had UFO sightings on the property and they do not broadcast it. I have had some very credible and highly respected people tell me their stories. Many of those individuals have been with others who all simultaneously saw an aerial anomaly. That is all I can say about that.

It certainly is true that anyone can see a UFO. A UFO after all is an unidentified flying object; it can be a bird, a plane, or Superman.

Did Bigelow give you any data or evidence from his investigations? Do you intend to release the evidence you collect?

[Fugal explained that absolutely no transfer of data or information was involved with the sale of the ranch. Bigelow has yet to make his findings public. As for my team, my scientists] will be working on releasing reports and information on a peer reviewed basis in the future. You know, in order for something to be properly understood from a scientific perspective, it has to be

characterized physically. You have to have repeatable results. It can't be anecdotal. It can't be random. There have to be physical laws that govern it, and right now, what we're doing is trying to gain a better understanding or a new understanding relative to the physical laws that are being challenged right now.

Sounds like BS to me. As mentioned earlier the idea of classification is nonsense. As for repeatability, the show introduces novelty every week. It would lack viewer interest of experiments were repeated. True, they give lip service to this, but don't carry it out.

It's strange. You literally buy land and build on it. Your career is heavily vested in developing buildings and building roots. Buying a ranch with so many stories about UFOs and monsters seems like the opposite of that.

One of the things I love most regarding the commercial real estate business is the privilege of seeing a tangible manifestation of my labor. To be able to see the results of the work and to put fingerprints on the literal landscape. In my line of work, you have to produce and execute precise physical results in order to succeed.

No, it's not the opposite of his career; it is his career. Following *The Curse of Skinwalker Ranch*, the tourist potential for the surrounding land is huge. It's like saying the introduction of a ghost ride at a funfair will scare people away – what nonsense.

***

Fugal, like many in Utah, was born into the Mormon church and considers himself spiritual. I considered the possibility that the Skinwalker

Ranch project was a personal quest for him; a quest for validation or for God. Don't we all have the tendency to explore and seek out the unknown? Perhaps this was Fugal's Bildungsroman, his journey into the unknown to seek adventure and, in some strange way, knowledge.

Looking over his shoulder, twenty-two stories up, my thoughts returned to downtown Salt Lake City, the skyscrapers and buildings Fugal has built his career around, and the massive church that loomed over the city. I wondered if he was truly driven by all the steel and bricks entrenched in the dirt that he was responsible for, or if his true passion and purpose was on a curious little ranch just on the other side of Utah's mountain range.

Joseph Smith, founder of the Mormons was a conman too. But folks fell for his BS, and have done so ever since. There is a sucker born every minute. While he may not be receiving anything from the *History Channel* by way of direct payments, the *History Channel* is the advertiser of this Area 51-Roswell expectation. The increase of tourism along with real estate capital gains is assured.

BRYANT ARNOLD, BA, AKA DRAGON

BA'S UNIFORM IS A BLACK SHIRT AND BLACK TROUSERS – We might also include the firearms he carries that appear to be props as much as anything else.

The designation of BA as *Dragon*, as fans will know, allegedly harkens back and is attributed to the manner of one of the ranch's security guards when Bigelow owned the ranch. Whether we believe the story that BA inherited this name in some curious fashion or not, the soap opera appeal of having the name of someone called *Dragon* as head of security makes for entertaining TV.

Little of BA's is said to be known. Both he and BF are said to go way back together. The photograph of them as Mormon missionaries decades ago begs questions of what their relationship was if any in the intervening time period. Despite a slight inference they go way back together and BA might be something of a *Mini-Me* to BF's *Doctor Evil*; this quote from *Celebs Fortune* however, shows the real connection:

It's been almost 30 years since they last met as teenagers in August 1992...[11]

One imagines the Mormon community is quite tight, like many other similar biblical groupings, and it seems likely to me that failing evidence to the contrary, their former association could have been one of many the two shared with countless others. We have no reason to disbelieve BA is not a crack shot as the programme indicates, and hunting trips feature him on social media. One wonders what BA's background is: is he landowning gentry or someone with a criminal record or neither? That none of his lifetime achievements are showcased indicates there are things about BA that are best not disclosed.

BA does not strike me as a security guard. In fact many with genuine security credential have questioned the way he carries and inadvertently points a rifle at people. In truth my local shopping precinct includes a couple of older fatter types that can barely walk. Nevertheless, most people with security antecedents charged with security work have far more muscular – nay fitter — physiques than BA.

This head of security fulfils an important plot device: namely among the triangle of the reluctant security leader against the go getting TT, arbited by the judicial BF who always seems to press ahead after voicing concerns. Like many in the Skinwalker Ranch team, one wonders how many may have had acting lessons.

I don't think you have to be a security expert to question BA's security credentials, but I do know of someone having law enforcement and security experience who has watched the show. Here is what Royce L Robertson writes on BA:

In my experience as former LE and Professional high level security company owner and operator I've worked with LE, Military and Security Contractors all over the world. Very wealthy people usually hire extremely well qualified individuals who do not exhibit the behaviors that this guy does. He exhibits outright fear and neurotic tendencies.

Being the lifelong friend of the guy who's running the show and "liking guns" is not being qualified! He has demonstrated extremely poor firearm safety and ordinary care. THIS demonstrates to me the lack of seriousness of the entire production.

Also no one there who knows anything about cattle behavior or knowledge of how a ranch works and should be operated.

For there to be a head of security there has to be other members of security. Kaleb Bench, KB is the other security team member we are made aware of. KB seems more stereotypically a security guy, having a large build. In front of the camera he speaks like you would expect security guy too, and the woodenness in the final episode as he speaks his script, exemplifies this.

I also wonder why there seems little if interaction between KB and BA on the show. Is it because BA's role is to escort BF the twenty yards from the helipad and be the *voice of doom*, leaving KB to actually perform something approaching a proper security function?

TOM WINTERTON, TW

TW's UNIFORM IS BLUE JEANS, A BLUE/GREY SPECKLY SHIRT AND A COWBOY HAT

&

JIM MORSE, JM

JM's UNIFORM FEATURES A BRIGHT WAISTCOAT AND A COWBOY HAT

TW is the *ranch superintendent*, and judging by social media, a firm favourite of the ladies. At this point I might reflect on the wisdom of why I wouldn't consider writing a book called *Why I Don't Like Boyband* -------- (fill in the blanks yourself). Of course, a show devoted to ostensibly uncovering mystery has morphed into a soap opera with most fans being none the wiser, yet the personalities have become a case of whether you like John, George, Paul, or Ringo the best. TW might be Paul, TT, John – and well, you get the idea...

The disproportionate number of men with no black folks whatsoever on the ranch might be something the production team might try to line up with current wokeness in the future. Although the need to maintain a masonic type business accord related to issues of real estate would be a difficult duck to line up with the cultural marxist benchmarks of mainstream media protocols we've all come to know and love.

Once again *Celebs Fortune* provides some interesting information:[12]

Thomas Winterton (birthday, March 5) is the superintendent of the infamous Skinwalker Ranch in the Uintah Basin of northern Utah. The Secret of Skinwalker Ranch cast member, like the others, is a close associate of the owner of the ranch, Brandon Fugal, and has also started his own company called Resonance Meditations, with his wife.

Aside from Resonance, he also founded Intermountain Economic Consulting, LLC, recently in January 2021 with an aim to create job opportunities with economic development in the Uintah Basin. He and his wife also founded a small chain of holiday homes in 2010, called the Winterton Suites, and remained its president until 2018. It's expanded to three different locations in Utah and North Dakota.

Once again, the real estate connection is interesting, belying the salt of the earth cowboy persona. Why does someone who deals in property need an income as a superintendent? We see TW in one episode tagging the cattle and driving an excavator. In this world of pseudo non-fiction, he is like a new kind of John Wayne. The viewer is led to believe that TW is a cowboy since wayback.

And if you are like me, you may wonder what a ranch superintendent is, considering that Jim Morse, JM is said to be *ranch manager*. One may wonder how to differentiate between job titles that seem like synonyms. Indeed they are.

One search reveals:

Manager is a synonym of superintendent.

Superintendent is a synonym of manager.

As nouns the difference between

superintendent and manager is that superintendent is a person who is authorized to supervise, direct or administer something while manager is (management) a person whose job is to manage something, such as a business, a restaurant, or a sports team.

As an adjective superintendent is overseeing; superintending.

***

Along with the most fantastic coloured waistcoats that JM possesses, as a more minor player in the Skinwalker saga, he too, rather than giving the image of living among native peoples, has a background in real estate. His rather portly physique suggests he is hardly of cowboy stock. Here is the beginning of one article on JM and others at the ranch:

He has over 30 years of experience designing and building complex experimental systems. Jim Morse is the Community Outreach Director for Skinwalker Ranch. The other team members include "principal investigator" Eric Bard, scientist Jim Segala, ranch superintendent Thomas Winterton, ranch manager Jim Morse, security guard Brent "Dragon" Arnold, and ranch owner Brandon Fugal.

Morse alleges that when the Utes and the Navajos came into conflict in the mid-1800s, the Utes cursed Skinwalker Ranch, and that started the supernatural phenomena. Mr. Morse began investing in real estate after an honorable discharge from the United States Air Force in 1973. As President of the company's subsidiary, To The Stars Inc., since 2015, he was primarily engaged within the entertainment sector...

I get the impression that JM is a bigger mover and shaker on Skinwalker Ranch than his few lines and appearances suggest. Given his entertainment antecedents, is he also part of the directing of the show?

Before he fell into opprobrium, the multitalented Australian Rolf Harris would paint impressionistic like depictions and ask the audience as he progressed, *can you see what it is yet?* Observing so many cast members having real estate interests in the Uintah Basin, is it likely they are promoting a vision of some sort of Area 51 cum Roswell theme park?

So, can you see what it is yet?

The prospect of renumeration from film production is potentially dwarfed by what tourist and real estate interests may bring in the long term.

***

Returning to TW, we must wonder about his famous head swelling claim. We see a picture of him looking miserable with a tube and bandage around his head. This was attributed to events on the ranch prior to *The Curse Of Skinwalker Ranch* filming began. I have several questions about this:

1/ Who wants to photograph someone in a hospital bed – including oneself?

2/ What purpose does it serve?

3/ Would he do it as selfie, or would his wife say, "Honey you look terrible – let me take a picture of you?"

4/ Where are contextual feature relating to this: the hospital room, staff and so on?

5/ Why doesn't he attempt a frail smile to try and encourage those who love him?

The photo is probably pure fabrication.

I had originally believed the actors while having certain scripts may have been targeted by real energy weapons and so were unwilling dupes. I cannot believe anyone among the cast if genuinely suffering from energy weapons would seriously attribute them to skinwalkers and UFOs rather than the military industrial complex. Even a person stupid enough to waste his time collecting six degrees wouldn't believe that. They have never speculated on the military industrial complex, and this too suggests a certain harmony with the fascistic corporate government nexus. I mean, why haven't they showcased perimeter fence footage seeking to rule out men in black with microwave weaponry?

This has never been on their radar, and so was one reason I initially entertained this idea. The sense that the team are all of one mind suggests conspiracy against the viewers' mindspace. So, ruling out UFOs, skinwalkers, and men in black, the simplest and most obvious deduction is that supposed personal radiation attacks are acted out. If half of what was supposed to be going was going on, the government would surely kick Hollywood scientists out and put real scientists in.

THE CARETAKERS OF HOMESTEAD ONE – KANDUS LINDE, KL, AND TOM LEWIS, TL

KL has a background in archaeology and anthropology. She is the co-author of the *Atlas of Human Cranial Macromorphoscopic Traits*.[13] Their Kindle book at the time of writing costs only £91.15 in the UK, or $100 in the USA. I'm sure many Skinwalker fans will now join the rush to complete their Skinwalker book collection.

Amazon reports:

Ms. Linde is an archaeologist, technical editor, writer, and freelance photographer. She received her B.A. in Anthropology from Utah State University, Logan. Her research bridges two fields:

anthropology and art, with a particular insight on photographing the nuances of the human skeleton. Her artistry spans many mediums, but she considers her son, Milo, to be her greatest masterpiece.

The book was published in 2018. She is clearly an accomplished woman — working as a caretaker(?) — and I wonder given her certain awkwardness in from of camera whether she is unhappy with what she is doing. The supposed strange noises and behaviour accorded TL's and her occupancy in Homestead One seem to have given little prominence other than their initial mention. I would not want to live in a property that *Mystery Inc* would want to visit; yet her evident unhappiness might owe more to the acting role she is playing than bumps in the night.

While KL's academic credentials are occasionally mentioned, the subtitle of *Caretaker* is seen more often than *Anthropologist*. Of course to credential too many on the show would deflate the big up needed for Mr Hollywood scientist himself, TT.

KL's relationship with TL is not so clear to the viewer, but may be inferred. They have been married for some time according to this article that interestingly doesn't say if she has children. This seems odd given her book bio affirms a son but neglects to mentions a husband. Probably of little importance, but just thought I'd point it out. When one is being deceived, little details might one day form a broader picture.[14]

Given KL's anthropological background I've wondered whether one reason she, may have initially been chosen for the show was to prostitute her academic background in some montage of Indian folklore, skinwalkers, discovered bones and so on. By the their own admission the Skinwalker team leave a lot of shot footage on the cutting room floor.

Appendix B – The Cast Of Players

Given her shy camera performances, she is not to the manner born, and so we don't know what performed script they may have disregarded from her. We have seen her get down into trenches with her trowel, but this aspect of her background as of the end of series two has not been leveraged so much.

***

TL, like his wife is also a shy character. It is no surprise KL has not taken TL's surname, given his friendly, inoffensive, and slightly wussy character. That he is not an ostensible alpha male may be deceptive though. Skinwalker Ranch is not just about the camera performances, it's about what goes on behind the scenes. Many fans on social media, assuming some reality to the place and say how they wish they could work on the ranch – how sad.

TL's background is in computers. I imagine that this pays far more than being a ranch caretaker. So by the producers own admission, the two caretakers are not ranchers – just like TW in fact.

I'm not aware of TL's IT skills being used in front of camera. With all the instrumentation and data collection, I find this odd. But here is some pure speculation on my part: I suggest that TL may liaise with EB. Who knows, perhaps TL configures the software to deliberately go haywire and display anomalous readings. I also make the observation that other than the Hollywood construct, TT, the programme makers tend to be cagey about the backgrounds of their players. Nevertheless, in so far as celebrity media can do background checks, the producers will not try and hide very obvious facts about the Skinwalker team that could be discovered elsewhere.

***

We don't see KL and TL interacting with the animals so much. BF has indicated in the show that he has known the couple for some time. KL's bio mentions she studied at Utah University. Once again, KL and TL could be part of a tight set of people who live in Utah. A common denominator of all those in Utah might often be the community of those professing Mormonism. I have no idea to what extent those folk not professing the main religion of the area are included or excluded from business schemes and so on. And life is too short for me to do a comparative study of the Church of Jesus Christ of Latter Day Saints, Judaism, and freemasonry. Knowing human nature, being in the same club will certainly open doors; as they say, *it's not what you know, it's who you know...*

RYAN SKINNER, RS –
AN OCCASIONAL SHOW GUEST

RS early on saw the grifting potential of Skinwalker Ranch. His marginal part in the filming suggests to me that on one hand they don't want to upset the applecart of the Skinwalker Ranch mythos by distancing themselves from him, but don't want to entertain his presence too much. His even wilder first-hand claims of phenomena if showcased too much might just be too much. People are said to be known by the company they keep. What does this say about BF and the rest I wonder?

RS is a one man BS factory on Skinwalker Ranch fayre. He has written eight books on the subject and boasts the largest Facebook group on the subject. After listening to his account in season two, episode two, I decided that I would read one of his books. It is of the pseudo non-fiction genre which I have come to loathe; clearly science fiction to those who can discriminate, it will suspend many readers' disbelief beyond what a fiction author has any right to. This is in the great tradition of course of P T Barnum who said, *There's a sucker born every minute.*

One book of his I read was, *Skinwalker Ranch – Path Of The Skinwalker*. It mixes up reality and illusion. We have no reason to doubt certain genuine biographical details. He describes his courting of his Ukrainian wife, Iryna. Assuming this isn't all fabrication, we learn from his casual comment:

Over the next year or so I made a couple of trips back, and eventually convinced Iryna to come with me to the States...

Who can afford to travel so much? Is he a qualified professional or person of independent inherited wealth? Why would a Ukrainian woman go back to the States unless he was a man of means. Authors usually don't earn that much; more so, since three of his books were published in 2021. He has clearly been riding on the coat tails of the TV series. This sounds like a man from a wealthy family. A wealthy land owning family perhaps? Omissions of his professional life demonstrate another non-barking dog among his tales of werewolves.

His Amazon biography gives:[15]

Ryan Skinner began his research into the phenomena at Skinwalker Ranch in 2006. Since the events chronicled in his books, he has returned numerous times each year to Utah's Uintah Basin to conduct field investigations. While there he spends his nights alone in the mysterious Utah desert, trying to find answers to whatever creatures lurk in the nearby mesas and valleys. In

September of 2009, Ryan created the web www.skinwalkerranch.com; a paranormal website which promote discussions on Skinwalker Ranch and other paranormal related topics.

In the spirit of adventure, Ryan has his Private Pilot's License, CDL, and is Scuba Certified. He graduated from Eastern New Mexico University with a Bachelor's Degree of Science and received a Major in Public Speaking and a Minor in Theatre. Mr. Skinner has written four other books, "Path of the Skinwalker", "NO TRESPASSING", "Tales of the Skinwalker", and "The UFO Farm". When not traveling across the United States in search of ufo hotspots and paranormal mysteries, you can find him enjoying time at home with his two children.

Ryan was featured as a "Paranormal Investigator" on 4 popular TV shows including Tru TV, Travel Channel, and History Channel. In 2021 he will be a featured guest on History Channel's "Secrets of Skinwalker Ranch". He anticipates writing additional true stories chronicling his future adventures and the harrowing tales of others who have experienced the paranormal.

As a producer, entertainer, adventurer, and author; Ryan Skinner hopes to continue his search for answers for many years to come, and invites you to watch him on his paranormal journeys. Ryan currently resides in Milton Wisconsin, where he lives with his two children, Whitney and Max.

You can view more pictures, stories and videos of his adventures and learn more about Skinwalker Ranch by visiting his website at: https://www.skinwalkerranch.com | Twitter: @SkinwalkerRyan | FB:

Anyway, returning to Path Of The Skinwalker, RS describes how he and his wife were chased by a orb along with seeing a couple of grey like entities. Here is a section that the reader can attempt statement analysis upon; underlined words are particularly illuminating:

> *I have to admit it was a surreal moment, as if <u>we were actors cast in some science fiction horror movie</u>. <u>Only there was no script</u>. Whether tragic or comedic, the fate of the characters was a matter of improvisation, one event linked to the next until the night played out. No one knew how it would end. But whatever was happening out there this night <u>was real and no movie.</u> There were <u>real consequences</u> for the people who had been in those cars. Iryna was right; we had to get the hell out of there. Thanks to her instincts and insistence, I am blessed to be sitting here at this moment able to <u>share this unbelievable, yet absolutely true story</u> with you.*

I don't even think you need to be conversant with statement analysis to ride a horse and cart through this. Suffice to say, the deep need to persuade put this firmly in the pseudo non-fiction genre. The reader might like to read the one and two star reviews on Amazon. I was generous and gave it two stars.[16]

And returning once more to the book content. From the road chase scene RS somehow finds himself inquiring of Skinwalker Ranch and eventually visiting. One Amazon book reviewer has already called BS on the distance of the road RS and his wife were on compared to the distance from the ranch. But he needs to be able to connect to the ranch with his narrative in order to slipstream with existing *canon*. RS writes:

> *I set out to research as much as I could regarding the location where the incident took*

place. Through various websites I learned that immediately to the south was a paranormal hotspot called Skinwalker Ranch. The Ranch, owned by a billionaire by the name of Robert Bigelow, was rumored to be a secret testing ground for the paranormal.

Here are excerpts from chapter twenty three, *The Skinwalker Cometh*:

> *The balls of light slammed into the earth some 20 feet from my foxhole. A rectangle of light crept across the ground towards me as if the door to a lit room had opened somewhere in the darkness. My eyes involuntarily turned away. Nonetheless, I forced them forward. My thirst for answers and my impudent curiosity were ready to welcome the madness, the paralyzing fear swept away. The answers were coming...*
>
> *From the darkness something stared back at me, watching me with terrible red glowing eyes. I awoke drenched in a pool of my own oily sweat. I knew that the monster from that nightmare had managed to look past the dream and into my world, the waking world. From across the dreamscape it saw me!...*
>
> *For the first time in my life, I stood unafraid to face the unknown. I felt the fearful child of my past blow away with the dirt beneath me as I walked confidently towards the light. The doorway had closed and something had come through. The black sheet of fog which had blotted out the stars and stained the ground began to suddenly collapse upon itself. It was a living cloth of darkness, its tentacles blacker than the surrounding night. Thick tendrils of living fog recoiled into a single point, twisting and spiraling as it did so. A miniature whirlwind of blackness spun before me.*

Appendix B – The Cast Of Players

From this spinning knot of darkness the Skinwalker emerged. Thick mangy hair bristled across a body that was much too large to be a mere wolf. It stalked towards me upon all fours. It eyes locked with my own. I was hypnotized by them. I was lost within their endless black depths; within them lay the secrets to the universe.

I stood transfixed and immobilized as they bore into me from a body that had no beating heart. I took a step forward, my newfound courage felt suicidal as I committed to the next step. Only a bird-brained fool would lack the common sense to sprint as far and as fast as his pumping legs would carry him to escape this living nightmare.

The eyes of the Skinwalker compelled me, called me and beckoned me forward. There was no breaking from its gaze. In that moment, I realized why I continued to advance. I was enacting my own nightmare with each step, replaying each terrifying scene as I drew closer and closer, my feet dragging across the sandy floor leaving behind a snake like trail, as if pulled by an invisible force.

I stood face to face with this traveler from beyond the stars, from beyond even time itself. I inhaled rapid gasps of air, keeping pace with the machine gun fire of my heartbeat. We were now pressed eye to eye, face to fang. To my relief, the wolf's glassy charcoal eyes did not erupt into flames, nor did it snarl or snap at my face. As my chest pumped like an overworked piston, I noticed the wolf did not take breath. It stood still like a lifeless statue of a medieval gargoyle, beautiful and foreboding.

A funny thought wrinkled its way into my brain. I had a sudden urge to reach out and touch its matted, mange ridden muzzle. My arm wavered *and inched up slightly, my fingers twitched with a palsied, arthritic tremble. I thought better of it, and kept my hand safely planted at my side.*

We stared at one another for what felt like hours. If there was an exchange of information, I was not consciously privy to the unspoken conversation. There was no smell, no sound, no lights, just the lifeless desert, myself and the wolf.

In a way that transcends written words, or even how we might imagine telepathy to be, the creature imparted its secrets to me. I instantly knew the knowledge it shared with me. It was as if those thoughts had always been locked away buried deep in my head...

To apply statement analysis to this would be to take a sledgehammer to crack a chestnut. Significantly, *The Curse of Skinwalker Ranch* production team have passed on the opportunity of mentioning this account of the ranch's apparent history. That RS has related other experiences on the ranch, is described in season two, episode two.

Suffice to say, BF has mentioned that RS has been a go between himself and the Shermans. The Shermans are a useful device since anything can be claimed on their behalf by people who claim that they know them. If the Shermans as far as their experiences are real, why entertain such an obvious hoaxer than RS.

Would you buy a used car off RS?

Appendix B – The Cast Of Players

1/ Travis Taylor
https://en.wikipedia.org/wiki/Travis_S._Taylor

2/ Radiance Technologies Appoint Travis Taylor
https://executivegov.com/2022/04/radiance-technologies-appoints-travis-s-taylor-as-principal-research-scientist/

3/ Cave Of The Crystals
https://en.wikipedia.org/wiki/Cave_of_the_Crystals

4/ The Missing Diary of Admiral Byrd – Fact Or Fiction
https://www.bibliotecapleyades.net/tierra_hueca/esp_tierra_hueca_20.htm

5/ The Inner Earth – My Secret Diary
https://www.bibliotecapleyades.net/tierra_hueca/esp_tierra_hueca_2d.htm

6/ Celebs Fortune Article On Erik Bard
https://celebsfortune.com/erik-bard/

7/ What Happened To Jim Segala?
https://www.reddit.com/r/skinwalkerranch/comments/nw5r26/what_happend/

8/ Facebook Groupies Discuss Segala
https://www.facebook.com/ancientaliens/photos/a.271665296208728/3679001365475087

9/ Celebs Fortune Article On Brandon Fugal
https://celebsfortune.com/brandon-daniel-fugal-net-worth/

10/ Interview with Brandon Fugal
https://www.vice.com/en/article/m7qxyx/brandon-fugal-owner-of-skinwalker-ranch

11/ Bryant *Dragon* Arnold
https://celebsfortune.com/bryant-arnold-dragon/

12/ Thomas Winterton
https://celebsfortune.com/thomas-winterton/

13/ Atlas of Human Cranial Macromorphoscopic Traits
https://www.amazon.com/Atlas-Human-Cranial-Macromorphoscopic-Traits/dp/0128143851/ref=sr_1_1?crid=21KZPH434S49G&keywords=Atlas+of+Human+Cranial+Macromorphoscopic+Traits&qid=1655491153&sprefix=atlas+of+human+cranial+macromorphoscopic+traits+%2Caps%2C762&sr=8-1

14/ Who is Kandus Linde?
https://information-cradle.com/kandus-linde-wiki/

15/ Ryan Skinner on Amazon
https://www.amazon.co.uk/kindle-dbs/entity/author/B00HGJMLPK?_encoding=UTF8&node=266239&offset=0&pageSize=12&searchAlias=stripbooks&sort=author-sidecar-rank&page=1&langFilter=default#formatSelectorHeader

16/ My Amazon Two Star Review : *I call this Pseudo Non-fiction*
https://www.amazon.co.uk/product-reviews/B00H9TFX2O/ref=cm_cr_unknown?ie=UTF8&filterByStar=two_star&reviewerType=all_reviews&pageNumber=1#reviews-filter-bar

APPENDIX C – STATEMENT ANALYSIS

BACKGROUND

My first contact with the discipline of *statement analysis* was from the work of Peter Hyatt; more specifically through work he was contracted to do for the British investigative journalist, Richard D Hall.[1]

Hall is a tenacious and intelligent individual. Among many other subjects he has applied his investigative skills to are the disappearance of Madeleine McCann and some of the bogus claims made by NASA.

Hall has employed Hyatt to scrutinise the speech of the McCanns,[2] as well as Neil Armstrong.[3] Suffice to say, to those who have looked at the McCann case, it is obvious that the McCanns know far more than they have said about the disappearance of their daughter, and those acknowledging the Apollo moon landing hoax know Neil Armstrong is a liar.

Of course, the fact that Travis Taylor of the Skinwalker team claims that Huntsville Alabama is *where rockets that travelled to the moon were built* already highlights Taylor as an idiot or a fraud.

More information can be found about Hyatt and statement analysis from his blog and also from his book: *Wise As a Serpent; Gentle As a Dove: Dealing With Deception*.[4] I want to give a brief summary of what Hyatt lays out in his book as far as it may be relevant to the Skinwalker Ranch deception.

I invite the reader to supplement their reading of the episodes where I refer explicitly or implicitly to statement analysis in order to achieve a more rounded appreciation of the subject. More than anything though, I strongly recommend reading Hyatt's book, as it is something of a Rosetta Stone in enabling the deciphering of the intentionally deceptive use of the spoken and written word.

I cannot claim any expertise in statement analysis other than reading the book multiple times. I have contacted Hyatt's site several times inquiring about the more formal courses they do. Alas, they have failed to get back to me. The book also includes an unfathomable number of typographical errors; something of a headscratcher since language is the subject matter of what it seeks to critique. OK, so no one is perfect...

WISE AS A SERPENT; GENTLE AS A DOVE: DEALING WITH DECEPTION – **SOME TAKEAWAYS**

Hyatt sets great store on what he calls the *reliable denial*. In what is reminiscent of the biblical injunction to, *let thy yea be yea and nay be nay*, Hyatt gives the first of the two statements below the hallmark of truth:

Appendix C – Statement Analysis

I did not steal the bag.

I did not steal the bag. I would never steal anyone's property.

The second statement is trying too hard to convince. For Hyatt the *reliable denial* is something of a gold standard for testing the veracity of statements. The second statement contains too much of a need to convince. Peter Hyatt writes:

The habitual liar feels a need to persuade and press the story. The truthful often speak in short sentences and lets the burden of belief fall upon the audience, and not upon the speaker.

Hyatt observes the importance of pronouns:

The pronoun is the single most focused indicator in Statement Analysis.

While he maintains that a person's vocabulary is often unique to themselves, pronouns are a real giveaway when conducting statement analysis. There should be no ambiguity. When someone is recalling a past event they well say *I* or they will say *we*. A confusion of the two is indicative of telling lies. Likewise, when a person uses the third person *you* to describe a past event, it is indicative of a fabricated happening. So, someone saying *I saw a UFO appearing through a portal* is more reliable than someone saying *You would see a UFO appearing through a portal*.

Hyatt observes that most of us, most of the time tell the truth. It is by omission rather than direct lying that truth is often hidden. The omission of personal pronouns in statements, he maintains, is indicative of untruth:

It should be noted that deception is often indicated in statements that begin without a pronoun.

Hyatt deconstructs the statement of fake hate victim Charlie Rogers who claimed:

Being a victim in a situation like this, or a survivor, um...

Another facet of speech that we are told to be aware of is the confusion of tenses between past and present. From what I can garner from Hyatt's writing, it is more reliable when someone uses the past rather than the present tense; the latter being more associated with fabrication in the *present* as it were. I would not wish to say anyone using the present tense to describe the past is necessarily lying, but it is something to be aware of.

And speaking of the past and present, Hyatt also teaches how to be observant of *missing time*; *missing time* is observed when someone under scrutiny uses such figures of speech as *the next thing I knew was that....* A sentence beginning with *And* is also said to indicate missing information.

*****

It is often said that a little knowledge is a dangerous thing. The few words in Appendix C are just a taster for a huge subject. I claim no expertise in statement analysis, but feel compelled to try and apply it to the Skinwalker Ranch charade. I invite others to try and get to grips with statement analysis as a tool that can be applied to BS detection beyond the scope of our current mutual interest.

1/ Richard D Hall website
https://www.richplanet.net/

2/ Statement Analysis Of Gerry & Kate McCann
https://www.richplanet.net/richp_search.php?ref=235&part=1&search=peter%20hyatt

3/ Richplanet 2017 Roadshow Video Diary – includes Armstrong statement analysis
https://www.richplanet.net/richp_search.php?ref=238&part=1&search=neil%20armstrong

4/ Hyatt Analysis
https://www.hyattanalysis.com/blog/

APPENDIX D – FACEBOOK AND FANDOM

BACKGROUND

The gullibility of the fans of the TV show has to be seen to be appreciated. This gullibility is reminiscent of the same public's stupidity in accepting the world scamdemic and poisoned jabs. The fans accept that people with paper qualifications as *scientists* are completely honest. The handsomeness of the players is somehow regarded as important in believing the week by week BS, and of course believing the team are all decent people.

There clearly is a vacuum of wanting to believe in something outside of themselves that ufology and related matters caters for. *The Curse of Skinwalker Ranch* is like a drug fix that fans suffer withdrawal symptoms from. Perusal of the various Facebook pages raises the same issues. One commonly asked question is why don't the cameras malfunction.

But why can't fans realise that the continuing promise of new discoveries will be no more than a dog chasing its own tail? The people besotted with the show do not want truth. They want to live in state of suspended disbelief that provides them escapism from the drudgery of daily life. Watching human beings indulge in this new deluded religion of reality TV, skinwalkers, and UFOs is extremely depressing.

THE FACE BOOK GROUPS

A large group is run by Ryan Skinner who links to his numerous Skinwalker books.[1] Here is one by Caleb Luker.[2]

But the best I've found is this one, and the one in which I came across the excellent analysis of Royce L Robertson. It contains a number of sceptics like ourselves, but we are still outnumbered by the number of female Travis Taylor groupies.[3]

This illuminating exchange took place that corroborated my suspicion about the Bigelow and Sherman relationship.

Royce L Robertson: *The Myers family never had any "stories". It wasn't until the Sherman's bought the place in 1994 and were losing money big time that all of a sudden, they came up with stories of the "paranormal". Funny if you dive deeper it appears that Robert Bigelow already knew the Shermans before they bought it.*

Simon Smith: *Have you got a link to that info please Royce?*

Royce L Robertson: *Most of it is in the above article.* [referring to the Garth Myers interview in the prologue of this book] *More comes from my personal interviews with government associates of my own.*

Simon Smith: *OK thanks. Do you see the Shermans themselves as the fabricators of Skinwalker "canon", or do you think George Knapp has been the "creator" of the various myths? How do you see the relationship between Brandon Fugal and Robert Bigelow ? I notice that BF has referred to RB as "Bob Bigelow", "Mr Bigelow", and "Bigelow" on the show. It seems that while BF has referred to RB as a "friend", for the purposes of the TV show he is unsure as how to regard or describe RB.*

Royce L Robertson: *All of that goes very deep.*

Senator Harry Reid, a Mormon, was one of the largest land owners in Nevada and was a friend of Bigelow, a Mormon. Reid was the primary Senator on the committee that allocated Black Money Pentagon, DOD projects. When an area became an interest to the government for top secret military experiments Reid and others would create a backstory about the properties and the entire area, protocol that precedes Reid and Bigelow.

This is a well-established process to contaminate the area with obscure stories and legends and make the general public attribute any unusual activity seen to the stories and legend. This takes time and needs to be perpetrated by third parties.

The Shermans, also Mormons, had a loose acquaintanceship with both Bigelow and Reid.(according to my sources). Again according to my sources, the Shermans bought the ranch with the intention of selling it to Bigelow and "unknown" partners.

They had no previous experience or knowledge of ranching and never profited from the ranch. The next step is for someone (Bigelow) to purchase a property, get awarded a lucrative Black

Money contract and allow government scientists to do their experiments, continuing to contaminate the public with stories of "strange unexplained " activity while lying about what is being looked at. On SWR it was never aliens or the paranormal.

It was always DOD weaponry. When finished, sell the property to a person who will participate in the promotion of the allegedly "phenomenon stories" as publicly as possible, allow that individual to profit as long as no disclosure is made. I believe that Fugal is that guy and the whole SWR thing is a continuation of the cover up. It has made it so that no legitimate or actual investigation can be done.

And I particularly like the below piece of analysis where Royce abstracts a template for the government modus operandi on such matters. It is sad that government lies to the people it is said to serve:

Royce L Robertson: There is a common theme that DOD follows for areas inside the U.S. to perform experiments that an outside contractor is necessary to avoid FOIA Act or open disclosure.

This happened in my area of East Texas and western Louisiana region years ago.

#1 Create a narrative about a specific property or region.

#2 Manufacture "evidence" through 3rd party testimonials, i.e.: "I heard, someone told me, I know or knew someone who saw.....etc.

#3 Perform tests with minimal interference due to "stories" influence.

#4 When finished, contaminate with disinformation about area and experiments by individuals "they" hire (contract).

#5 Area begins to be infected with true believers seeking to "find proof" and justify their theories and beliefs.

#6 Encourage those individuals to completely confuse the masses so that no one can ever get to the real truth.

#7 Continue to monitor the area and create sporadic incidents to further the original narrative.

***

The extent to which the majority of the various Skinwalker group members are prepared to contort reality in order to retain the air of mystery in their life is astonishing. They are in fact hypnotised by the TV that continually promises resolution. This is in fact the same psychological device that has been used for hundreds of years by unscrupulous preachers who prophecy that we are living in the end time *now* – that everyone previously had obviously got it wrong.

This expectation of the *Second Coming* in Christianity is mirrored by the promise of *Disclosure* in the *UFOs-must-equal-ETs* religion. One doesn't have to be a Marxist — and I'm certainly not — to recognise that religion is the opium of the people; that organised religion has always been a political device is hardly to be contested by philosophers. Seneca said:

Religion is regarded by the common people as true, by the wise as false, and by the rulers as useful.

And in the final analysis it will be impossible to convert people of faith to people of reason. It was impossible in Seneca's day, and it is impossible now.

Appendix D – Facebook And Fandom

1/ Ryan Skinner Facebook group
https://www.facebook.com/groups/481151978650301

2/ Caleb Luker Facebook group
https://www.facebook.com/groups/370124607484820/

3/ The Most objective Facebook group
https://www.facebook.com/groups/1687428964648601

APPENDIX E – *SKINWALKER RANCH IS A GRIFT*

BACKGROUND

I came across the video and transcript of *Answers With Joe* that I give below. I believe *The Curse Of Skinwalker Ranch* is more than just a grift, it is a scam that seeks to realise real estate capital gains for many with an interest. Joe makes some very good points, although he is ultimately far too kind to those he is critiquing. Here is the transcript of the video. [1,2]

TRANSCRIPT

Growing up, my grandparents had a ranch. They raised and sold cattle, harvested oats and hay, collected farm dogs by the dozen. It wasn't anything fancy but it was a pretty cool operation. They weren't alone either, there are over 2 million farms and ranches across the United States as of 2019 anyway. Most of them you've never heard of.

Some are more well known for being historic or just for being huge like the XIT Ranch and the King Ranch here in Texas. And then of course there's ranches like Skywalker Ranch, home of Lucasfilm, and Southfork Ranch, home of the Ewing family from the show Dallas. And then there's Skinwalker Ranch, home to... well, according to legend, scary humanoid creatures, mutilated livestock, ghosts, giant unkillable wolves, electronic disturbances, and UFOs.

It's almost like an amusement park of the paranormal. Or about 15 X-Files episodes in one spot. But if we're being pedantic, it's not famous because of what's happening there. If you've heard of Skinwalker Ranch, it's because at one point or another, you've run into the endless barrage of media about this place. Books, movies, feature documentaries, podcasts, several episodes of popular TV shows, and starting last year, a reality show that's now finished its second season on the Ancient Aliens channel. Sorry! The History Channel. I keep forgetting they still call themselves that. And that show is super popular, its finale ranked number one for that time slot.

Without a doubt, Skinwalker Ranch is a valuable commodity at this point. Regardless of what's actually happening there, it is pulling in tens of millions of dollars. And of course, I've received tens of millions of requests for a video it. Because my UAP video was... Universally beloved. But you know what, it is an interesting story. And if nothing else this has become a pop culture phenomenon and I kinda want to know how we got here.

So how did we get here?

All good mysterious places have a mysterious backstory. It's kinda like architecture, you need a good foundation you can build the spooky on top of. And Skinwalker Ranch is a place that seems ready-made for the spooky. Skinwalker Ranch is located in northeast Utah in the Uinta

Basin. It's close to Ballard, Utah, and consists of 2.1 square kilometers (512 acres), though some sites list it as 1.9 square kilometers (480 acres) in size. It was owned by the Myers family from the early 1930s to 1994.

They sold it to cattle ranchers named the Sherman family, and in fact the property is sometimes still referred to as Sherman Ranch. The Shermans only lived there for two years before selling it to billionaire businessman and aerospace executive Robert Bigelow. Bigelow is famously a believer in UFO phenomena and wanted to study the area after hearing about some of the Sherman's experiences on the property.

Bigelow owned the property for twenty years, during which time the land was investigated by his group, the National Institute for Discovery Science (NIDS). But in 2016, Bigelow sold the property for $4.5 million to a shell company called Adamantium Real Estate, who immediately shut down all roads to the ranch, lined the property with barbed wire and installed security cameras around the perimeter. But maybe the most telling clue about what their intentions were with this ranch was when they trademarked the name, Skinwalker Ranch, in 2018. Within a year a feature documentary about Skinwalker Ranch was released and production had begun on the now wildly popular – and lucrative – History Channel series.

Could I sound any more cynical right now?

All right, now would be a good time to disclose that I am severely biased on this subject. I've been pretty open about my disdain for reality shows and the manipulation of reality that they engage in, I talked in a very early video about Duck

Dynasty and how the guys in that show were non-bearded middle-class dudes before they got cast in this show, and then got rich selling a bunch of merchandise. That's the grift. And it's happened with a lot of reality shows. So yeah, the fact that this has a reality show around it immediately sets those alarm bells off for me.

But... Is that true here? Is the guy behind Adamantium Holdings running a grift? Well let's look at the guy behind if. His name is Brandon Fugal, and he's a real estate mogul and VC investor out of Utah. Fugal had a religious upbringing in the Church of Jesus Christ of Latter-day Saints, which is a fancy way of saying he grew up Mormon, and according to interviews with him, this is what spurred his interest in the paranormal. The idea that he could have proof that there's more out there in reality and in the universe than what we can see, this would be the ultimate validation of his faith. But he's an interesting guy, he owns a huge movie memorabilia collection, is passionate about 80s music, and collects supercars like Lamborghinis and Porsches. He has also joined an investment group that plans to resurrect the wooly mammoth.

Fugal told Utah Business in 2020 that he purchased the ranch as a skeptic, believing that there would be natural explanations for all the strange activity. But, "What we are witnessing could be evidence that we live in a multi-dimensional universe," he said. "That we are not alone. That we may be interacting with other entities, other intelligence." Fugal hopes that discoveries on the ranch prove that we humans are part of a greater plan, that we're not just a random event and that there is meaning to our lives and existence. And you know what, honestly, if he's sincere about that, and he seems to be... Hell, I'm down for that, that sounds great. The question becomes, how does making a lucrative reality show out of this further that effort? Is it just because it generates interest that might bring in more researchers? Do they plan to reinvest the money being made on it back into the research? Is it a have-your-cake-and-eat-it-too kind of thing?

I want to note that we did reach out to Mr. Fugal, who responded at first but when we asked him that specific question, we didn't get an answer. He may have gotten busy; I'm sure he's a busy guy, don't want to make wild accusations, I'm just letting you know we did try to cover our bases and get his side of the story.

All right, so let's talk about the Ranch itself, what's the deal with this place?

The Uinta Basin is the geological remains of the prehistoric Uinta Lake that formed in the late Tertiary period about two million years ago. The basin is surrounded by the Uinta and Wasatch mountains and the Roan and Book cliffs. It is up to 10,000 feet above sea level and covers more than 9,000 square miles. Prehistoric sites show that it was inhabited thousands of years ago by the Archaic and Fremont peoples, and then more recently by the Ute tribe.

Fathers Dominguez and Escalante were the first Europeans in the area when they traveled through in 1776. Brigham Young sent out a small party to explore the basin in 1861 as a possible place to settle, but the party reported that the area was valueless. Abraham Lincoln created the Uintah Indian Reservation that same year, and gilsonite, which is a kind of asphalt was discovered in the basin around 1888.

The land contains oil, too. It has more than 8,000 gas wells and 2,000 oil wells, with mineral rights being the primary income source for the Uintah and Ouray (you-ray) Indian Reservation. Then there's fracking, which has been occurring there since the 1960s. And this comes with a few issues. A Rolling Stone article in 2015 concluded that the ground air in the basin was "fraught with carcinogenic gases like benzene, rogue emissions from oil and gas drilling."

The high levels of volatile organic compounds has been floated as an explanation for the number of livestock that get sick and die in the area. Even Fugal is cautious about the emissions, saying "I have four kids but they have never been to the ranch," he told Utah Business. "The danger is real and we have to approach the ranch with a degree of reverence and caution." A lot of the lore around Skinwalker Ranch comes from the indigenous tribes that inhabited the area for hundreds of years.

The Uintah and Ouray Reservation stretches across three counties in the basin. It's the second-largest Native American reservation in the U.S., covering 4.5 million acres. Anthropologists say the Utes migrated to the northern Colorado Plateau between 1,000 and 2,000 years ago. The Utes are talented artists, specifically known for their religious and ceremonial beadwork and leatherwork.

In their religion, they trace their origin to a half-man, half-wolf god named Sinauf (sin-oy-uff). They also believe that all the physical elements and features in the world are spiritually alive. Their oral history includes sightings of strange creatures in the basin, and they take the area very seriously.

According to UFO investigator Junior Hicks in an interview with George Knapp in 2002, "They think the Skinwalkers are powerful spirits that are here because of a curse that was put on them generations ago by the Navajos," "The Utes say the ranch is 'the path of the skinwalker.'"

So what is a skinwalker exactly? Well, according to lore, skinwalkers are malevolent witches who can transform into a wolf, bear, coyote, bird, or other animals.

They're known to the Navajo as Yee Naaldlooshii

Legend says that skinwalkers are often shamans who have crossed over to the dark side by participating in forbidden rituals and ceremonies that summon evil forces. So I guess if shamans were the Jedi, Skinwalkers are the Sith. Belief in skinwalkers is still pretty strong among the tribes in the area, in fact, most won't talk about them because it's thought that saying their name kind-of invokes them. They're kind-of he whose name shall not be spoken.

With that history and legend behind it, the list of unexplained phenomena that has been reported at the ranch is quite extensive, including...
– Cattle mutilations
– Sightings of strange, humanoid figures
– UFOs
– Light beams hitting the basin
– Poltergeist phenomena
– The appearance of portals
– Balls of light
– Radiation blasts
– Electronic malfunctions

While claims of UFO sightings in the Uinta Basin go back to the 1950s, most of what we think of as the Skinwalker Ranch phenomena started when the Shermans took it over in 1994. For example, the Shermans found a dead cow in a field after one of the UFO sightings on the ranch. They told the Deseret News in 1996 that there was "a peculiar hole in the center of its left eyeball but was otherwise untouched with no trace of blood." There were no traces of footprints, predators, or tire tracks. A chemical-like odor was also present. Another dead cow with a similar hole in its left eye was found later. There was also a 6-inch hole about an inch deep carved out of the cow's rectum, along with the same chemical smell. What is up with aliens and butts?

Anyway, cows began disappearing, more were found mutilated, crop circles were discovered, metallic sounds were heard at night, strange creatures were consistently seen, and orbs darted around the property. For example, Terry Sherman saw a blue orb moving across a field. His dogs chased after it into a thick grove. He heard the dogs yelp and then silence. He went back in the morning to look for the dogs and saw three spots of dried grass. A greasy, black lump was in the middle of each spot, looking like the dogs had been incinerated.

If you're interested in reading more about their experiences, I'll put some links down below.[3]

So as a guy with two dogs, I think if something like that happened I would want to get the hell out of there, and it seems that was true for the Shermans too. Which is why after only 2 years on the property, they sold it to Bigelow. Which makes you wonder, if the place was so freaky that the Shermans yeeted out of there after only 2 years, what did the Myers family see? They owned the *property for 60 years. And the answer to that question is where things get really weird because what they saw... Was nothing.*

Kenneth John Myers and his wife Edith sold the land to the Shermans and they're not with us anymore but Kenneth's brother, Garth Myers, claimed that they never saw anything paranormal there. He spoke to Frank B. Salisbury, PhD, who published a book called The Utah UFO Display, and said, "There was nothing, unequivocally, absolutely nothing that went on while [Edith] and my brother lived there" And he claims that after the Shermans sold the ranch, Bigelow called Garth and asked him why he never told anyone about the UFOs. And according to the book, he responded by saying, "I told him they [the UFOs] didn't get there until [the Shermans] got there." Yikes.

So look, the skeptic in me sees a ranch with the Myers family living there for 60 years, nothing happening, just an old family ranch, and then the Shermans come in and suddenly there's all these random stories of paranormal events going around, they get tied in to ancient native lore, they use this to get an eccentric billionaire to buy the property, making a huge profit, and later Adamantium comes along and does the same thing, just generations of people profiting off of this story.

But... the wrench in that theory is that the Shermans only sold the property for $200,000. It's actually less than they paid for it, they took a loss on this. They moved away and have refused to talk to anyone about their time there. Possibly because of a non-disclosure agreement they signed with Bigelow. And there's nothing really from their past that would indicate that they would do something like this. Terry Sherman was a well-respected *breeder of top-quality and high-priced cattle in New Mexico before buying the ranch in Utah. He never lost more than one percent of his animals per year until he moved. This loss of cattle hit the family's finances pretty hard. And whatever else was happening caused them all psychological stress.*

Now if you wanted to double down on the cynicism you could argue that Terry Sherman wasn't doing quite as well breeding cattle as he had been and his reputation and pride were taking a hit so he conjured up these stories as a way to sort-of save face. But it is weird that the people who set this whole scheme into motion according to the "grift theory" are the people who profited the least from it. One more thing worth mentioning is the issue of digging on the ranch. This is something they talk about in the series, they have an aversion to digging because apparently, digging disturbs the entities on the property, causing all sorts of physical phenomena to occur. But could the no-digging suggestion stem from something more mundane? Remember that the Uinta Basin is loaded with fossil fuels like gas and oil and asphalt, well according to Garth Myers, the real estate contract stipulated that the previous owners retained oil rights on the property.

In other words, if someone were to dig around and find a bubblin' crude, that would belong to the previous owners. So... They don't want you doing that. Again, that's Garth Myers' theory, another one has to do with the high level of VOCs in the area I mentioned earlier. It's possible that digging may release them and may even be the cause of some of the claimed medical issues seen on the show. Yet another reason one might not want to dig is because there may be radiation in the soil from the nuclear weapons tests in Nevada between 1951 and 1962.

It's thought that fallout from those blasts landed in Utah, specifically in that area. So yeah, digging might stir up some ancient spirits... or radioactive dirt. Neither of which sound like a fun time. So we've talked about the Myers', we've talked about the Shermans, and the current owner, now let's talk about the one, the only, Robert Bigelow, paranormal gigolo.

For the record, I like Robert Bigelow, I think he's got some cool ideas. A little kooky, but that's fine. So Bigelow bought the ranch in 1994 and then set up the National Institute for Discovery Science in 1995, specifically to research this place. And they did so for 20 years. So what did they find?

One thing they experienced was an ice circle that mysteriously appeared in 2002. The circle measured five feet nine inches in diameter and was found in an irrigation canal. The circle was 1/4-inch deep. Shavings around the circle indicated that it had been etched into the ice. There was no evidence of melted ice. There were no markings, tracks, or prints in or around the circle, either. The case went unsolved.

And there were some other things they ran across like weird bits of metal and electronic disturbances and stuff, I'll put a link in the description to an archive of their findings, as well as things they investigated outside Skinwalker Ranch. But I actually kinda lied just a second ago when I said they investigated for 20 years. Technically that's not true. NIDS was actually disbanded in 2004. But it was replaced with another group called the Bigelow Aerospace Advanced Space Studies, which was an even more secretive operation. And nobody really knew what they had going on until this year.

Remember back in the Spring of this year when all the UFO stuff came out about the secret government program investigating aliens and whatnot? That program was AATIP, the Advanced Aviation Threat Identification Program, and a smaller part of that story if you followed it much was that Robert Bigelow was working with them in some way. Which wasn't a surprise to me, he's super into that stuff, but this was what he was doing for that program, he was investigating Skinwalker Ranch.

Also Harry Reid, the senator who pushed to fund the program, he's a friend of Robert Bigelow. (Maybe put in a caption on screen AATIP was budgeted at $22 million and lasted from 2004-2012) Bigelow's advanced space studies operation lost its funding in 2012 when the Defense Department shut down AATIP. So Bigelow's researchers had government funding for 8 years to study Skinwalker Ranch, and it would be great to know what they found... But it's classified.

And after that research kinda stalled. He just kinda owned the land for a few years. Until, it seems, somebody got an idea for a TV show.

So look, here are the prevailing theories around Skinwalker Ranch:

– A shaman is trapped in an alternative timeline and is causing havoc.

– The ranch is a portal for interdimensional travel for beings and UFOs to pass through into our world.

– The U.S government made contacts with extraterrestrials, but they're trying to cover it up.

– It's a spot for extraterrestrials to study us and

our reactions to their presence.
– It's a scam perpetrated by the Shermans,
Bigelow, and Fugal to make money.

Bigelow has been researching this kind of
stuff for a long time, he's legitimately interested in
this kind of thing, and talks about it all the time.
He's risked his career publicly talking about it. And
it's very possible Brandon Fugal is exactly the same.

He may legitimately want to research this
stuff, but research costs money, and he wants it to
be well-funded. So, we'll make a reality show out of
it. It's compelling stuff, people would want to watch
it. He's not wrong about that. Maybe this is one of
those cases where the scammy thing to do and the
smart thing to do are the same thing. Hell, maybe
he was inspired by the Mars One program.

Mars One was a privately funded program
to take people to Mars and the way they were going
to pay for it was by making it into a reality show.
The idea was people would do research and
establish the Mars base and do all the science stuff
but they'd make a reality show at the same time. It…
didn't work out very well. But being a businessman,
I'm sure he was able to run the numbers and see
that this would have a better chance of success than
Mars One.

Despite what you may have heard, it is
easier to get to Utah than it is to get to Mars. But
yeah, we'll make a TV show and do all the stuff
you've gotta do on a reality show to keep people
watching, but we'll do some real research while
we're at it. And who knows, maybe we find
something, that would be huge!

I am willing to give the benefit of the doubt
here. Maybe that's exactly what Fugal is doing. I'm
still not sure if it's the best way to go, but at least his

intentions are pure. I guess we'll just have to see where all the money goes. But you know what, it's well done. They did a great job with it. It's fun. And I mean, reality shows aren't my thing, but a lot of other people enjoy them. In fact, I'm sure this show was a nice escape for a lot of people over the last couple of years. When we all kinda needed one. Man, I can't believe I'm defending the Skinwalker Ranch reality show. I really didn't think I'd land here. Shhhhhhhhit.

Honestly, I came into this video really ready to throw down, this was going to EXPOSE THE FRAUD. And here I am. Defending it. Ultimately, they're making entertainment. And on the off chance there is something really funky going on there, it increases the odds of finding it. So I don't know what do you think? Good thing? Bad thing? Dumb? Any favorite scenes from the show? Discuss your favorite theories in the comments...

1/ Skinwalker Ranch Is A Grift – Article
https://answerswithjoe.com/skinwalker-ranch-grift-said/

2/ Skinwalker Ranch Is A Grift – Video
https://www.youtube.com/watch?v=oZEdcyWF6VA

3/ Collection of Links Given In Article
https://www.deseret.com/1996/6/30/19251541/frequent-fliers
https://studylib.net/doc/6968873/article-in-spirit-magazine-terry-sherman-speaks
https://rense.com/general32/strange.htm
https://rense.com/general32/utah2.htm

APPENDIX F – DISCREPANCIES IN CANON

BACKGROUND

I want to examine some discrepancies between the alleged happening on the ranch as reported by George Knapp and Colm Kelleher, and those reported by supposed witnesses in the TV series. When one appreciates how huge these discrepancies are, one wonders how they have got away with their BS for so long. A simple answer maybe that we live in a self-actualised idiocracy that watches far more TV than it reads. In any case, I invite the reader to discover more discrepancies between the show and *Hunt For The Skinwalker* for themselves, beyond what I give here.

CONTRADICTIONS

The first contradiction I want to draw the readers' attention to is the season two, episode three, featuring John Alexander, JA. Not only does his testimony not cut the mustard in term of statement analysis, but differs from the written word here:

"I'm not goin' to let him get another calf," Tom snarled as he suddenly ground the truck to a halt and reached behind for his rifle. We were no more than fifty yards from the large creature that lay motionless, almost casually, in the tree....

"Got him," yelled Tom triumphantly. "I saw him fall to the ground." We scrambled back into the truck and Tom stopped about forty feet from the tree. There was no sign of the large creature under or near the tree. We split up and searched for any sight or sound of the wounded or dead beast. Thirty yards to my left Gorman suddenly yelled, "I see him." The shout was quickly followed by two loud reports from his rifle. "Got him at point blank," Gorman yelled as we jumped excitedly over the fence into the thick undergrowth. The snow crunched loudly underfoot as we stumbled around looking for some sign of it. We were cautious because a large, wounded animal was especially dangerous at night.

I was still carrying my video camera as we warily looked all around, half expecting something to spring at us from the darkness. But there was utter silence.

"He jumped back here when I hit him," Tom said as he scratched his head in puzzlement. "I was no more than forty feet away. Where'd he go? That sucker must have weighed four hundred pounds."

We began quartering the area, looking at the snow for tracks. Something that big should have left an obvious trail in the snow and there should have been blood. It was then that I saw it—a single, obvious oval track about six inches in diameter embedded deeply in the patch of snow. I yelled at the other two, who came running. I shone the flashlight, and there it was. It looked unusual: a *single large print in the snow with two sharp claws protruding from the rear of the mark going a couple of inches deeper. It almost looked like a bird of prey, maybe a raptor print, but huge and, from the depth of the print, from a very heavy creature. I began videotaping, as the physicist unsteadily held the flashlight while looking over his shoulder, waiting for a large wounded animal to charge us.*

Minutes ticked by as we searched in vain for a companion print. We found another one in an area of unmelted snow about twenty feet from the first, but nothing else. We listened carefully for any movement in the undergrowth as we searched.

And here I give again part of JA's interview when he gives an online interview to the Skinwalker team:

Some of our people who are out late at night; this is in the winter, and they look up and there's something up in the tree; looks like it's above one of the cattle...

One of our guys has a rifle with him and shot; whatever it was fell out of [he hesitates here] *the tree* [we know the creature is in the tree; JA is trying to be overly consistent IMO] *and disappeared totally* [Why the emphasis? *totally,* is redundant and indicates a need to convince.]

They went out the next day — I said it was winter and there was some snow on the ground — the one thing we found was this track that looked like a gigantic raptor... [undecipherable] *something out of "Jurassic Park" kind of raptor print, and we couldn't find any other tracks whatsoever* [once again, why the redundant *whatsoever*?]

The reader might notice that in the book they search at night, but according to Alexander as interviewed, they look the next day. Some of his defenders might say that just because he said, *they went out the next day,* it doesn't mean they didn't look at night. But the truth is, the older account contains the supposed information recovered by flashlight at night that Alexander said was discovered in the morning.

***

The second account difference I want to look at is in the account of a Sherman nephew, whom the TV show in season two, episode five tells us is *Steven Wall, SW.* TW tells us that SW lived for four years on the ranch. One wonders how his schooling could have been achieved if that was the case...

Since the Sherman only lived on the ranch as owners for less than two years, it is also difficult to see how four years divides into two years as well. Chapter eight of, *Hunt For The Skinwalker,* informs us that the Sherman nephew came to the ranch in 1994. And bearing in mind the authors' use of nom de plumes, *Dave* would be Steven:

Around the same time, Dave, Tom's nephew, had arrived to visit with the family for a few weeks...

Dave's stay would be cut short. His parents let the family know that the youngster would not return to his cousins while they still lived on that property in Utah.

SW's account of his UFO encounter is different from in season two, episode five as well. The book says:

Suddenly a loud gasp from the boys made him look up. The RV was now definitely in the air. All three stopped to watch. With the red light on its tail, it climbed smoothly, slowly, and silently toward the top of the tree line. Those trees were more than fifty feet high. As the object crested the tree line, the bewildered trio saw the shape of the vehicle perfectly silhouetted against the horizon. It was no RV. The object was roughly oblong, shaped like a large refrigerator, with a headlight in front and a red light behind. All three watched in complete silence as the object slowly disappeared over the trees in the distance. It was flying smoothly and slowly, almost casually. There was no sound....

And it is worth repeating what SW said in episode five:

When I was a kid, me and my uncle saw something coming down off from the mesas. As we were we standing by the house, there looked like bouncing ball and orb, I guess you would call it.... it was like a blue colour. I remember hearing the dog whimper, and then I remember finding the dogs SMASHED. I don't really know what happened, but I just know man couldn't do that.

And here where I point out that the book doesn't mention a portal at this point.

The first story that I can <u>really really hardcore remember</u>: down there there's a gulch [a vee shaped valley] ..OK...right over there <u>you could see something</u> open up there in the sky...something came out of it; a peach coloured object, OK. Me and my uncle saw it come through the field.

But, it came working its way up through [he points and sweeps around] *them Russian Olive trees and it came up and just scouted these trees just like this. It came up, went over the canal and it drove down the path of that road right there...*

And here I reproduce the dialogue between TT and SW on the demise of the three dogs:

SW: *They weren't vapourised, they were compressed into the ground...*

TT asks further...

SW: *Like something heavy smashed them* [He accompanies with his foot coming down, and downfaced palms pressing down.]

The book says:

Three large circles of brown, dried-out grass were in the middle of the clearing. At the center of each circle of shriveled vegetation was a blackish greasy mess. The stink of his incinerated dogs was awful. Tom rushed out of the copse, his mouth dry and his stomach heaving.

And so again I submit that while vapourised and incinerated are not necessarily perfect synonyms, the different observations between dogs being killed by heat or squashing, needs some explaining. Not only that, Sherman's nephew wasn't even on the ranch when the dogs were killed according to the book. If the producers of the TV series can't do their due diligence on checking out simple things, it means they aren't interested in doing so.

***

A third discrepancy I give is more of a reimagining of a previous fiction. It is clear that those promoting the fictions of Skinwalker Ranch have been keen to try and establish anomalous phenomena occurring before the Shermans and experienced by the Myers, who were unfathomably able to put up with the ranch's misbehaviour for up to sixty years.

I believe I have detected an occurrence that the book mentions occurred during the Sherman's ownership that has been reinvented for extrapolation prior to their ownership to suggest the Myers experienced these kinds of things. *Hunt For The Skinwalker* speaks of Tom and Ellen Gorman — *aka Terry and Gwen Sherman* – having four bulls disappear. Here from chapter sixteen:

Tom walked around looking at the footprints in the corral. The animals had been there only forty-five minutes ago. Ellen was sobbing in the truck. His search meandered over to an old small white trailer located at the west end of the corral. There was no entrance to the trailer from the corral except a door that was tightly locked and hadn't been opened in years. As he passed the trailer he glanced in. Tom froze. All four animals were standing silently, crammed into the tiny narrow, confined space

Now, in the TV series, Kris Porritt, the retired sheriff, describes a similar scenario with Ken Myers:

What happened right here was one of the biggest tricks you ever seen in your life... Ken couldn't find three heifers. I got here just at sunrise with my horse. We rode all day long. I said "Ken, I don't know what to tell you about your heifers. We can't find fresh tracks, and he had a shed right here [he points], *and Ken couldn't get the door open...so they start pushing on it, pushing on it...I pushed as a hard as I could to the inside, and I looked in here ...and I looked inside and said "Ken, you ain't gonna believe this. Your heifers are in the shed..."*

They were stacked one top of each other like this...[demonstrates with fingers]...

So even if you believe these were genuine separate incidents, my question is:

Do human beings tell lies or do paranormal-ETs-skinwalkers etc have nothing better to do than confine cattle into small spaces?

INDEX

Index

Index

ABOUT THE AUTHOR

Simon Charles Smith is a mathematics and physics graduate, ex teacher, retired councillor, county level chess player, and author of the bestselling *Fake Aliens And The Phony Nuke World Order*. The combination of fields involving education, politics, and analytical study, have uniquely endowed him with the wherewithal to deconstruct those with agendas misleading the public...

Printed in Great Britain
by Amazon